A Pocket
Full of
Miracles

A Collection of Heartwarming True Stories

Don J. Black

Covenant Communications, Inc.

Covenant

Cover images ® 2000 PhotoDisc, Inc.

Cover design copyrighted 2000 by Covenant Communications, Inc.

Published by Covenant Communications, Inc.
American Fork, Utah

Printed in the United States of America
First Printing: May 1989

07 06 05 04 03 02 01 00   10 9 8 7 6 5 4 3 2 1

ISBN 1-57734-649-1

A Pocket Full of Miracles

*For Ann, who is constantly enriching my life,
and our children Tosh, Celestial, Crysta, and Tyler,
who continually show us examples of righteousness.*

Table of Contents

Preface

I love the Gospel of Jesus Christ. Countless times I have given thanks for my turn on earth and for the many times Heavenly Father has manifested His kind hand in my behalf.

Once, many years ago as I was driving, the thought suddenly came to mind, "How do you know that the gospel of Jesus Christ is true?" Before I could question further, my mind began to flood with warm, detailed evidences of my knowledge of the truthfulness of the Gospel.

The first one to enter my mind was the origin of the Book of Mormon. If Moroni didn't direct Joseph Smith to the hiding place of the original gold plates, and if the Lord hadn't blessed him with the power to translate, how did it come to be? The more my mind contemplated the question, the more it filled with obvious answers. Another evidence came to mind—patriarchal blessings. "What church, not possessing total truth, would dare to make such daring claims through personal blessings to its worthy members?"

My mind continued to build a case of evidences with such questions as, "If it's not true, then explain the many experiences and little miracles you have personally enjoyed through direct answer to prayer, or the joy of understanding the plan of salvation."

In this book, it is my desire to share with the reader a portion of the joy and a few of the miracles I have experienced through the influence of the great gospel of Jesus Christ.

It is my sincere hope that someone, somewhere, will grasp the vision of this writing and that it will kindle hope, love, and the warm feeling of testimony of the truthfulness of the gospel of Jesus Christ.

Sincerely,

Don J. Black

Chapter One

Sweet Miracles and the Priesthood

". . . the rights of the priesthood are inseparably connected with
the powers of heaven, and . . . the powers of heaven cannot be
controlled nor handled only upon the principles of righteousness."
(D&C 121:36)

I've often thought about and tried to comprehend how gracious and unselfish our Father in Heaven is to share with us the sacred power of the priesthood—the holy, personal power of God. It is difficult to find adequate comparisons in this mortal life.

Could it be compared to a father who allows his sixteen-year-old son to use the new car? Or to a young intern given full responsibility to perform delicate surgery? Perhaps the closest earthly comparison is when a newborn is placed in its mother's arms, with God entrusting the very life of His child to her.

Perhaps every man endowed with the sacred responsibility of the priesthood and the great power of this trust, identifies with the thought, "Who am I to be entrusted with such holy power?" Feelings of deep inadequacy often fill me as I ponder a blessing, an anointing, or other uses of priesthood power. When this power is used to bless others, the priesthood holder can come closest to his Father in Heaven.

One of the first times I called upon the power of the priesthood, I was a young missionary serving in the coastal fishing port of Esbjerg, Denmark.

It was late afternoon, and my companion and I were presenting a discussion. Suddenly there was a knock at the door. The man of the house answered and motioned for us. There stood a sister from the local branch. She informed us that another member, Sister Riis, was seriously ill and needed our help immediately. We excused ourselves, hopped on our bicycles, and pedaled quickly across town. Sister Riis was lying on the couch. She was breathing with difficulty and was in a semi-comatose state. Further, she didn't seem to realize we were there. Because we were young and didn't have much experience with the priesthood, we weren't sure that a blessing could be given to someone who was not fully conscious.

Nevertheless, we knelt down by the couch where Sister Riis lay. Together with her son and the sister who had come for us, we offered a prayer that Heavenly Father's holy spirit would attend this sacred occasion. We did feel His spirit. I recall the sense of childlike humility I had in response. My companion and I administered the blessing, and Sister Riis turned on her side and entered into a deep, restful sleep. We left, feeling peaceful about the events that had transpired.

That evening as we closed the day with prayer, we felt the same sweet spirit again. It was a wonderful learning experience.

The following morning we were eager to learn of Sister Riis' condition, and stopped by her home first thing. When we knocked at the door, an energetic voice called, "Come in!" We did, and there stood Sister Riis. Her son had told her about the previous evening's ordeal, and about the blessing we had given her. She was obviously delighted as she exclaimed again and again, "I feel good. I feel wonderful. I have never felt so good."

My companion and I were astounded at the dramatic change in the woman's condition. We felt that, as a result of exercising the power of the priesthood, a miracle had taken place. Our testimonies grew.

NETWORK OF SPIRIT

Some years after, I had another memorable experience involving the priesthood. A couple in our ward had just learned that their infant daughter had a serious disease characterized by mental retardation. I offered consolation and asked if there was anything I could do to help. The father, worn down with sorrow, said he would like me to help Brother Johnson, a member of the ward, administer to his baby.

Before leaving my home to give the blessing that night, I knelt in prayer and took inventory, recalling the past week, the days, the hours and the minutes. Then I drove slowly to the young couple's home. Brother Johnson and I arrived at the same time. I had great respect for Brother Johnson, a man who had a lot of wisdom sprinkled with goodness and common sense.

We met each other on the walkway to the front door where we shook hands and discussed the responsibility awaiting us. His faith was comforting. Approaching the porch, we could see the father sitting at the dining-room table, his face buried in his hands. When we entered, we saw his wife in the kitchen doing dishes. Their little boys lay on the floor watching television, apparently unaware of their parents' grief.

We walked down the hallway to the back bedroom where the infant lay. The father reached into the crib, picked up his daughter and held her close. His wife wept quietly as we administered the blessing. During the blessing there was a sense of peace and comfort that all would be well.

Upon returning home I decided to call my seminary students to ask them to join us in fasting and prayer. As I asked one girl to participate, she replied, "Can I finish my dinner first, Brother Black?" (My heart warmed at her sweet and innocent reply.)

There is great strength and power when a group of Saints unite in faith and prayer for a common cause. We all fasted, and the following afternoon as we joined together in prayer we felt the unmistakable warmth of the Spirit.

Three or four days later, early in the morning, I received a phone call. It was the father of the infant. When I recognized his voice, my mind came to full attention and I quickly asked about his daughter's condition. The father's voice was full of joy. He informed me that follow-up blood tests had been taken. "There is no sign of the disease in my little girl's body," he announced. He cried with joy and I cried with him. We felt sure there had been divine intervention on behalf of that child.

The following Sunday, the father of the little girl was asked to offer the benediction at sacrament meeting. As he walked slowly to the pulpit, a very special spiritual overtone was suddenly felt. There was an unusual hush, even though the folding wood chairs on the old board floor were rarely silent.

The teenagers who had joined in the fast were sitting in that congregation. These teenagers knew something big had just taken place in their lives, but they were unaware of the father's knowledge of their fast and prayers. By chance, he had heard several youth talking about the situation outside of the chapel earlier in the day. When he took his place at the pulpit, he bowed his head, paused, then lifted his head again. Looking about the room he saw the faces of those teenagers looking into his. In that moment a powerful spirit overcame everyone involved. Tears filled the eyes of the young father, as well as the eyes of each teenager. A spiritual network was felt, connected to the same source of power—the holy priesthood.

OH, HOW LOVELY WAS THE MORNING

Svendorg, Denmark is a lovely coastal town located at the southern end of the middle island of Fyn. It lies approximately forty kilometers from the village of Odense, the birthplace of Hans Christian Anderson. It is an area as rich in beautiful waterways and islands as it is in historical significance. Sister Andersen was a woman in her sixties who had never married, and her body revealed the painful swelling of arthritis. Early one morning we were summoned to her home. She planned a visit to the doctor that afternoon, and desired a priesthood blessing. We placed our hands upon her head and administered the blessing. When we had finished, Sister Andersen looked down at her foot, lifted it slightly, and moved it back and forth, exercising her ankle. When tears filled her eyes, we wondered why. "Look!" she exclaimed, pointing at her ankle as she moved the foot back and forth. "That joint of my body has been in a tightly locked position for forty-five years. But look at it!"

We did look, and rejoiced with her. As missionaries, of course, we were to stand at arm's length from all members of the opposite sex, but suddenly this grand woman grabbed us and gave us the biggest hug and squeeze we'd had since our moms kissed us goodbye at the train station. The three of us stood there embracing and rejoicing in the miraculous power of the priesthood.

Help From Above

When I was preparing to leave on a mission, several things concerned me. "Who am I," I wondered, "to go out into the world to teach people who probably have more experience than I?" It was a humbling thought. What if my knock at the door brought me face to face with a person of superior intellect: a doctor, lawyer, or minister of another faith? As the actual departure time drew near, my worries increased. Finally I talked with my father about it all.

My father was a man of few words, but he was wise. He looked at me and said, "The Lord works in mysterious ways, my son. Stay close to Him. Stay worthy and at the moment you need an answer, you will be given it by the power of the Holy Ghost." At the time I didn't understand the depth of what he said.

Before long I found myself knocking on the doors of thatched-roof homes in Denmark. Little did I realize I would soon experience the reality of what my father had shared with me.

We were invited into a home one day by a young man who listened to our message with great interest. In our conversation we learned he held a doctoral degree in chemistry and anatomy. We discussed many things, including the revelation about the Word of Wisdom. Realizing we were approaching his area of expertise, I felt a little inadequate.

He asked me to explain why tobacco was harmful to the body. I cautiously felt my way through the conversation, indicating that the nicotine content in burning tobacco caused damage to parts of the respiratory tract, as well as other parts of the body. Referring to section 89 of the Doctrine and Covenants, I further explained that tobacco was to be used in caring for sick animals.

"You don't appear to be aware of the body's biological need for nicotine," he said.

"Need?" I asked slowly.

He reiterated the statement with great confidence. I felt lost for a moment. What can you say when all the knowledge you have to fall back on are the lessons you had in Primary? Then I remembered the words of my father, "At the very moment you need an answer, you will be given it." I needed answers, and the Lord knew it.

To my surprise, the following simple testimony came from my lips: "The Word of Wisdom is from God. Therefore it is true. Because the Lord told us tobacco and nicotine are not good for the body I know they are not good." It was easy to say, yet seemed too simple to be a solid, hard-hitting intellectual reply.

Surprisingly, the man suddenly changed his entire approach, and a sweeter look came over his face. "You're absolutely correct," he said. "I was just testing your knowledge on the subject. The amount of nicotine the body needs for correct sustenance is automatically found in normal foodstuffs."

That day I learned the truth of a statement often quoted by President Harold B. Lee: "A testimony is when your heart tells you things your mind doesn't understand."

DOCTOR OF THEOLOGY

A similar experience took place in the presence of a doctor of theology and religion. It was awe-inspiring to reveal truths to him that he had never heard before: answers to questions regarding man's destiny, where man came from, why he is here, and where he is going.

It was especially thrilling to give such basic truths to a learned man. Just a few months before, I was the one the mission president had asked to find 2 Nephi in the Old Testament! And I tried to do it, only to quickly find that the joke was on me. I was thankful at that time and every day since for a loving and patient Heavenly Father and the Holy Ghost to help me.

TINY GIFTS OF TONGUES

My companion and I were in the process of presenting the gospel to a young woman and her fiance. She was from Denmark, and he was from Germany. She had previously enjoyed several discussions and was enthusiastic for her visiting friend to hear them. This particular discussion included the Word of Wisdom, and there was a good spirit present. But as we related more details of this principle, the young man became alarmed. He emphatically began defending his belief of drinking wine.

It was an interesting situation. We would present the topic in Danish, she would translate it into German, her fiance would respond in German, and she would then translate his conversation into Danish. Our minds would then quickly translate it into English!

The conversation became more and more intense. Points were being made and accepted and it was an important moment. Then a small miracle began to take place. Waiting for the effort of translation to take place, my mind suddenly began to comprehend what the young man's reply was, prior to the German-to-Danish-to-English translation. I was amazed because I'd had no exposure to the German language. It was a small sip from the sweet cup of our Father in Heaven's spiritual greatness, and a glimpse of how He will help us if we try to live and spread the gospel message.

Chapter Two

Life's Purpose and God's Caring

"For behold, this is my work and my glory—to bring to pass the immortality and eternal life of man" (MOSES 1:39)

I share the following story with the permission of my longtime friend, William T. Garner. It is told in his own words.

"While a young jet fighter pilot with the U.S. Marines in Korea, I was assigned to lead a four-plane division on an air-support strike in the north. The weather was marginal, and in returning to our field it was apparent that we had to fly close to the ground to stay below the heavy clouds which were continuing to build. The airstrip was situated on the east coast of South Korea at the mouth of a large bay and, because the terrain was mountainous, approaches to the field in poor weather were generally made over the bay. This practice permitted aircraft to fly under the clouds and keep the field in sight.

"On this occasion, however, as we reached a point approximately ten miles from the field, flying at an altitude of approximately three hundred feet, the base of the clouds suddenly dropped and we had virtually no visibility. I immediately began a shallow climb and informed the field that we would have to be brought in on a ground controlled approach (GCA). Then, after determining that my section leader (the number 3 aircraft) and his wingman (the number 4 aircraft) had slightly less fuel than my wingman and me, and because the GCA is too dangerous for more than two aircraft at a time to attempt, I ordered my section leader to take his wingman and himself in first while my wingman and I flew a course and altitude as directed by the GCA controller. We would do that until it would be time for us to make our approach to the field. My section leader complied, and we assumed different headings.

"The situation was delicate but not particularly unusual. Then, suddenly, my radio transmitter ceased to function, and, because a transmitter is essential to lead a GCA approach, I instructed my wingman by hand signals to assume the lead and I took up a position on his wing. My receiver was still operative, and we continued to fly at altitudes and headings as directed by the FAA controller until the other two aircraft could be brought down safely.

"My indicated airspeed was perhaps 350 knots (nautical miles per hour) when it happened. Although we were in the clouds, I suddenly saw a mountain immediately ahead of me. Instinctively, I snapped the control stick back, applied full power, and began what must have been a vertical climb, completely losing sight of my wingman.

"I climbed until I broke out on top of the clouds at approximately 30,000 feet. Meanwhile, I heard on my radio that sudden, violent storms had closed every landing field in South Korea. I knew there was a field called Ki near Pusan on the southern coast of Korea, and felt that if I headed due south the cloud cover might not extend far beyond the coastline. I thought I might have a chance to fly to the edge of the cloud layer, descend to a few feet above sea level, turn north and fly just over the water back in the direction of K-1. Although it was a long shot, it was the only apparent choice.

"As I continued south, I realized that my fuel was nearly gone, and, when I reached a point where I believed the south coastline to be, I saw that the clouds continued to the south as far as the eye could see. My plan hadn't worked.

"Then I decided I would have to eject and hope I would either reach the ground or water safely, or be rescued before the Korean winter killed me, although I knew there was little likelihood of that.

"It was at that instant I saw immediately below me a small hole in the clouds and, through the hole, 30,000 feet below, the landing strip of K-1. Without taking the time which a proper descent requires, I did a 'split 5,' extended my dive brakes, and headed *straight* down for the field. My approach was terrible and I landed much faster than the book permits, blowing both main tires in the process. But I landed and I was alive. My fuel tanks were empty and when I looked up to find the hole through which I had just flown, it was not there.

"My former wingman was never seen again, and I have never since heard of a hole going through the full thickness of clouds which extend from ground level to 30,000 feet.

"The most important aspect of this incident, as far as I am concerned, is that while I was heading for the south coast with several minutes to contemplate what seemed to be the probable end of my life, I remembered my past irresponsibility in my relationship with my Heavenly Father. It was then, under the most difficult of circumstances, that I began to realize and feel the great anguish of one who has squandered his time and talents—who has failed to use this life as well as he might have done. I resolved that if I had a second chance I would live so that such regrets would be unnecessary. I was fortunate enough to receive that opportunity, and I pray I will always remember the lesson of that experience."

We all have such turning points in our lives. Times we realize what life is all about—that, really, we owe everything to our Father in Heaven, and always will. When we realize these truths that King Benjamin declared in his immortal address, we become more pliable in the hands of the Lord. We become better instruments in His hands, and therefore more susceptible to the promptings of the Spirit. One such instance occurred while I was serving on my mission in Denmark.

To Lisa from Heavenly Father

My companion's name, at the time, was Elder Don Coleman. He was a fine man and a fine missionary. We used to joke about who was the senior companion, as we couldn't recall which one of us departed the ship first when we landed in Copenhagen, Denmark. We solved the dilemma by taking turns with the senior companion responsibility.

Our field of labor was on the northern tip of Denmark on the island of Vensyssal in the town of Hjørring. It was referred to then as a two-man town. The two of us had most of the responsibilities. One Sunday evening for sacrament meeting, Elder Coleman had greeted at the door while I played the prelude music. He then took his place at the stand and conducted the meeting. I played the opening hymn and sacrament hymn, and helped pass the sacrament. It was also my turn to be the main speaker that evening.

Now, new missionaries often called upon some secret assistance when delivering a talk those first few times. We didn't realize that most of the members present recognized the "secret" immediately. The secret consisted of slightly modifying a discussion and giving it as a talk from the pulpit. I suppose every missionary thought he discovered the idea. I did, and was about to present mine on the subject of the Book of Mormon.

When Elder Coleman announced my name as the main speaker, I stood and immediately placed my notes upon the small podium. I had written the entire talk/discussion in phonetics, to better assist me in reading the still very difficult Danish language. I began with the words *"Gode aften min kaere søskerne og venner.* (Good evening my dear brothers, sisters and friends.) *Det er godt at vaere her med jer.* (It is good to be here with you.) *Iaften, vile jeg gerne tale om . . .* (This evening, I would like to speak about . . .) At that moment, prior to telling them the subject of my talk, there was a disturbance in the back of the old hall where we met. Because of the creaking wood floors, and wooden folding chairs, it didn't take much to cause a disturbance. I looked up for a moment and noticed a teenage girl taking her place in the congregation. Her name was Lisa. She sat down as quickly as she could. In that momentary break, however, as I looked down again at my notes, very suddenly the deeper, more sensitive part of my spirit heard the still, small voice. It said distinctively, "That young girl who just entered does not need to hear another discourse on the Book of Mormon at this time in her life. She needs to hear a strong testimony on the importance of living a virtuous life. Teach her the law of chastity."

To my great disadvantage, I had never heard a strong testimony about chastity. Secondly, the natural man within me wanted to immediately *leave* the stand and find someone more qualified to fulfill the responsibility. But simultaneously came automatic movement of my left hand. I pushed my prepared notes to the upper-left corner of the stand. I took a firmer grip on the edges of the pulpit and leaned slightly on one elbow for extra stability. I suddenly commenced upon this most challenging assignment. It was one of those moments when all doubt is removed as to the origin of the text, as one is literally carried by the Spirit and the power of the Holy Ghost. It became one of those circumstances indeed, as President Marion G. Romney reported, "I always know when I've spoken by the spirit because I learn something from what I've said." The discourse commenced, and I must confess was one of the best I had ever *heard.* It was even *masterful.* There were times during the presentation that I couldn't wait to hear what I was going to say next. No one was more thrilled or listening more attentively than was I.

At the completion of this miraculous event I took my place on the stand, prior to moving onto the organ bench for the closing hymn. Elder Coleman, who I might add, was a very reserved, almost dignified sort of fellow, leaned over to me and whispered, "Do you know how long you spoke?"

I said quietly, "Fifteen minutes or so?"

He said in a serious and slow fashion, "Forty-five minutes, in a foreign language, on a most difficult subject, without notes." Then he reached his hand over to me, shook my hand and congratulated me. I couldn't believe it. It was a lovely and miraculous event in my life.

But the wonderful miracle was not over. When the closing hymn was announced and I began playing it, I glanced over at Lisa. The hymn was "I Know That My Redeemer Lives." I noticed she had taken a hymn book in hand. But she did not sing, and after the first few stanzas, her emotions broke. She bowed her head, placed her hands over her eyes, and began to weep uncontrollably, like a little child. Then the true meaning of the preceding miracle became evident to me. The special message in my talk was directly from Heavenly Father to his own daughter, Lisa. He just asked me to deliver it. And I did.

Just One Little, Lost Girl

Not too long ago, I was summoned by a good friend. His little granddaughter had not returned home from school. I don't think I will ever forget the look of concern on his face when he said, "My granddaughter is missing. Will you help?"

Several of us volunteered to look for her. We set out to scan the neighborhood. Men drove slowly up and down streets. One man on a motorcycle weaved in and out of parks and yards.

I drove to the school, parked, and searched every area of the school yard. I looked behind the bushes, trees, crossing tunnel, and every other place imaginable. Coming upon one large shrub, and peering through it, I thought I noticed a little bundle nearly obscured from view.

I looked closer, and my heart pounded with fright, realizing what the sight could be. I pushed away heavy branches, and upon the ground sat two little boys. They were as surprised as I was. They convinced me they knew nothing of the little, lost girl, but were just having an innocent game of hiding from the world. I hurriedly continued my searching.

During the next few hours, many thoughts flashed through my mind. Here in this city were several men out looking for one little lost girl. Our hearts felt the almost sickening feeling of what could be involved. Oh, how we all wanted to find that child. We wanted her safe and unharmed. My thoughts went to our Father in Heaven, as he must look down each day upon the earth and witness hundreds of his beloved children becoming lost, mistreated, and harmed. I prayed, "Oh Father, let her be safe. Help us find that little, lost child."

We continued our search. Nothing seemed more important than finding that little child. Later I drove to my friend's house to check on the latest developments. He bounded out the door and greeted me with a broad smile on his previously forlorn face. "We found her! She's safe!" he exclaimed.

Oh, the feeling I experienced cannot be expressed. "She's safe!" My entire body sighed, yet trembled with gratitude. At that moment my spirit bore witness of the scriptures: "Remember the worth of souls is great in the sight of God;" (D&C 18:10), and "if it so be that you should . . . bring, save it be one soul unto me, how great shall be your joy with him in the kingdom of my Father!" (D&C 18:15). God cares about each one of his children more than we could ever comprehend.

Chapter Three

Righteous Womanhood: Channel of Light

*"For this cause ought the woman to have power on her head
because of the angels. For as the woman is of the man, even so is the
man also by the woman; but all things of God."*
(1 CORINTHIANS 11:10, 12)

*"Husbands, love your wives, even as Christ also loved the
church, and gave himself for it."* (EPHESIANS 5:25)

Whenever I teach section 89 of the Doctrine and Covenants, I
stress verses 18 and 19: "And all saints who remember to keep and do
these sayings, walking in obedience to the commandments, shall . . .
find wisdom and great treasures of knowledge, even hidden treasures."

What an expanded dimension of love and blessings! The Lord
promises His children that if they live this principle, they will be
blessed with good health—not only physical health, but spiritual and
mental health as well. Is it any wonder that we see along life's busy
pathway those occasional little miracles that take place within our
own families?

My wife and I have enjoyed several experiences along this line
throughout the years of our marriage. One such incident took place
some time ago. We were to have a Family Home Evening that afternoon, beginning with the family bicycling together over to a nearby fast-
food place. We were going to take the lunch we purchased to a secret
family spot in a nearby forested area for a good old-fashioned picnic.

My wife Ann and I were standing together in line waiting to buy our food, each holding a little one in our arms. Our oldest daughter, Celestial Dawn, and our oldest son, Tosh, were playing. Suddenly Celestial came up to me, pulled my shirt, and poked my arm in an obvious attempt for attention. I looked down at her and said, without really *seeing* her, "What do you want, honey?" A split second later, though, my eyes focused on her face. Her lips were turning a bluish color, her face was going pale, and there was the unmistakable look of panic in her eyes.

She couldn't answer any of my hurried questions, and the fear on her face remained. I exclaimed, "Ann! Something is wrong with Celeste!" Ann instinctively took over, telling our daughter, "Open your mouth, honey, open your mouth wide." She obeyed immediately, but we could see nothing obstructing her breathing. I had the sinking feeling that we didn't know how to help her, when suddenly, Ann placed her finger down deep inside Celestial's throat and with a distinct hooking motion, flipped out a marble. I was amazed. "Ann," I demanded, "how in the world did you know about that marble?"

"I didn't know," she answered. "It was as though I was led to do what I did, even before I could reason things out."

Almost immediately, Celestial recovered from the frightening ordeal. We recovered somewhat later.

That night as we knelt together for prayer, Ann and I offered special thanks for a loving and watchful Father, and for a sweet and timely miracle. We had literally felt and tasted from the cup of "wisdom and great treasures of knowledge, even hidden treasures." How grateful I was for a wife whose worthiness was manifest in the receiving of inspiration in behalf of our little one.

A MOST HELPFUL AND UNDERSTANDING COUNSELOR

I'll not soon forget the day I was called in to meet with my stake president. He got right to the point, drawing his chair close to mine and asking, "Brother Black, is there anything amiss in your life that would prevent you from honorably serving the Lord?" His second question was equally direct: "Are you morally clean and totally faithful to your wife?" And the third question also involved my wife. "Will Ann sustain you in any calling you might receive?" I said that she would.

We returned to the room where my wife and the rest of the stake presidency were waiting. At that point the stake president called me to serve as a bishop.

Ann and I were stunned. We looked at him momentarily in disbelief, and then at each other. We were then told that it would be our task to help create a new ward at Brigham Young University. This additional responsibility didn't alarm us initially, as the shock of being called as a bishop was still in effect. We would find out later how much work is involved in creating a new ward.

The stake presidency then ordained me a high priest and set me apart as a bishop. The shock of the call kept returning, bringing with it feelings of inadequacy. One passage in particular from that blessing comforted me greatly. The stake president said, "Now I encourage you to listen to your wife for added understanding, inspiration, and help. She will be one of your most helpful and understanding counselors." At that moment the Spirit bore witness of the truthfulness of this comment, and I silently vowed to take it to heart.

As we left the stake presidency's office, the awesome task of organizing a new ward began. My first responsibility was to choose counselors. Many names came to mind, but were all dismissed for one reason or another. The task was suddenly much greater and more serious than I had ever imagined. In the following days I continued in prayer and fasting. My wife joined with me. It seemed I would finally feel good about a particular man, only to learn he was moving out of the area or was being called to another position. Then, after some days, one name kept returning to my mind. Parts of past conversations came back to me and I had a vivid recollection of certain incidents involving this man. I remembered his ability to work with men on the high council, his knowledge and expertise in working with people in general, and his courage in standing up for a cause. I felt sure he was supposed to be one of my counselors.

But the second name just would not come. Then one day, driving down the street, Ann turned to me and said, "I know who your other counselor should be."

"Who?" I asked, curiously. When she told me the name, I was taken aback. We hadn't even seen the man she named for five years. But I learned he had recently moved back into the area, and when I sought confirmation, the Spirit bore witness this was, indeed, the second counselor I had been searching for.

The evidence of the divine nature of the call of these two counselors was not only manifest to me by the Spirit prior to their calls, but was seen when our new team went to work. Never in any previous calling had I experienced more closeness, love, and mutual dedication.

Blessed inspiration—from the power of the priesthood and the spiritual sensitivity of womanhood. It's an unbeatable combination.

No Giving Up

The school year was just beginning. It was a time when students identify with teachers and vice versa. In my last class of the day, five students—one boy and four girls—decided to put me on their "hot list" for some reason.

From the first day of class, the notorious five caused constant distractions. Talking, whispering, note writing, reading other material, and interrupting, were typical of their daily behavior. One girl even placed her desk sideways in the aisle. When I asked her to change it, she uttered a sarcastic, "No!"

Hard days became harder, and trials became catastrophes. I was losing and didn't like the feeling. I prayed. How I disliked the idea of ousting from class those students who were obviously the ones who needed help most.

Two long weeks passed without any changes. Finally, after counseling with the principal, a decision was made. I would present the five students with the ultimatum that unless they made drastic changes immediately, letters would be sent to their parents, school principal, and bishops indicating that they had been dishonorably released from seminary.

The threat didn't faze them. At the end of class, I again retreated to my office and prayed. Deep disappointment filled my soul as I returned home that afternoon. Ann asked what was wrong, and I told her I wanted to quit teaching. She didn't say much about it, and we spent a quiet evening together.

That night I climbed right in, but my wife knelt patiently beside the bed. "Shouldn't we pray?" she asked.

"I don't really feel like praying," I answered. But seeing her kneeling alone made me feel guilty, so I quietly got out of bed and knelt next to her.

"Would you like to say it?" she asked.

"No, thank you," I responded.

"That's fine. I'll say it."

Now, Ann has always been one to pray the way she feels. There is no vain repetition with her. She began her discourse that evening by saying, "Heavenly Father, Don thinks he wants to quit teaching—again. But we know he is just tired, and doesn't really mean it. Please bless him to rest well tonight and feel better in the morning. Help him to know that the kids who don't like him need his help the most. And please bless those kids to know he really does love them so they will understand, and love him too and let him teach them."

I slept well that night.

A couple of days following this experience, I again found myself standing before that class, with the notorious five coming in the door. I assumed they would take their usual places at the rear of the classroom, but they didn't. Instead, they made their way to the front seats on the front row. Students in the class watched in amazement. So did I. I suspected the worst. I asked the class to open their journals and was greatly surprised when five journals on the front desks were snapped open.

I thought to myself, There they go. It's a play for mockery. I paid no attention, determined not to give them the satisfaction of disturbing me, if that was their motive. I proceeded to write the material on the board for the students to copy, glancing out of the corner of my eye to see if there was any chance they were copying the material. They were!

We continued, and so did they. At the close of the period, class was dismissed, and I turned to erase the board. Looking around me, I took sudden notice of the five still sitting in their places.

"What do you want?" I asked.

"We want to know about our church," said one.

I quickly replied, not intending to let them get the best of me, "Come on, what is it you *really* want?"

"We would like you to teach us about our religion."

"How much do you want to know?" I asked.

They said they'd missed it all along the way and now wanted the "whole thing." I couldn't believe it. They really wanted to learn about the gospel. So even though the official school day was over, I went quickly back to work. As I taught them, they listened intently. We closed this first impromptu session with tears in our eyes, and made an appointment for another session the next day after school.

Suddenly I wasn't so anxious to quit teaching. At the close of the following day the same five remained in their seats and we began our second spiritual discussion. Several days of such sessions followed. Grades improved and unhappy expressions changed. The five had found the Gospel of Jesus Christ and were applying it in their lives, and they radiated happiness.

Years later, I ran into the young man who had been one of the changed five. He informed me of one detail I had not been aware of. He told me that just prior to the change in their attitudes, they had been conspiring together on their next approach of disturbance, when strangely and suddenly, each of them began to feel wrong about the whole situation. He said a feeling of not wanting to do bad came over them. "And that's when we made up our minds to change," he recalled.

I love those kids. And I love my good companion. I was ready to quit, but she wouldn't let me give up. Without her support and encouragement, I would have missed out on many rewarding experiences in my teaching years.

MICHELLE'S COURAGE

At the commencement of the school year, I always made it a practice to give the kids an in-depth lesson about the plan of salvation. This armed them from day one with an added understanding of their personal identity, their reason for being on the earth, and a purpose for maintaining that identity. It took nearly seven days to complete the lesson and to answer all the questions that inevitably arose.

When the segment of the lesson regarding final judgment was discussed, I told the classes that certain types of sins, such as stealing, lying, swearing, or experimentation with drinking or drugs, could usually be taken care of with the person or persons offended, and with the help of our Heavenly Father.

I then told them that if the offense was one of a sexual nature, it was necessary to visit personally with the bishop and to be guided through specific steps of repentance. Often, during this part of the discussion, a hush would come over the room. In these sacred moments, I could tell at a glance those who were in need of help and were taking this lesson of life deeply into their souls.

Following one such lesson, a girl named Michelle lingered behind when class was dismissed. She was a lovely girl, but her clear blue eyes were clouded with tears of hurt and worry.

"Are you all right, Michelle?" I asked. She turned around slowly, her eyes toward the floor, and said in a broken voice, "No, I'm not. Your lesson hit hard." She paused momentarily, looked over at the board, and continued, "My boyfriend and I have committed many of the moral transgressions we've discussed. There is only one thing really left, and that is the final act. I know if we continue in the same activities it won't be long. We're losing the battle, Brother Black. I ache and hurt throughout my body and spirit. I cry myself to sleep every night." Then in total humility, she added, "Will you help me?"

"What do you want me to do, Michelle?" I said quietly. "I am not your bishop. You would have to see him, you know."

"I know that," she said. "I mean, help me get the courage to stop. Will you pray for me?"

"Have you prayed for yourself?" I asked.

She seemed surprised at my statement, and said, "No."

"Why not?" I asked.

"Because I don't feel worthy. I'd feel like a hypocrite."

"A hypocrite? How would praying make you a hypocrite?"

"I don't feel like Heavenly Father wants to hear my prayers when I am a sinner," she said. "That's why I won't pray."

"If the sinners don't pray, my little sister, who does?" I asked gently.

Michelle looked up again, a look of discovery on her face. With renewed hope she asked, "Will you pray *with* me?"

"I would love that," I said. We went into my office and knelt there together. She asked if I would pray first. I did. I told Heavenly Father that two of his children were kneeling before him, and asked if he would help his sweet daughter. During that sacred communication, Michelle began to weep. Six months of feelings were suddenly released.

She had cried herself to sleep many times previously, but without hope. Now the tears were tears of hope. Following my prayer, she prayed. At last, the six-month silence was broken. Michelle was again on speaking terms with her Heavenly Father. Help and happiness were on the way.

"Tell Ron the times of intimacy are all over," I said.

"I will," she promised. "I couldn't before because he always hurt my feelings by saying, 'If you love me, let me.' Now for the first time in these many unhappy months, I feel strong enough to tell him."

"When will you be able to?"

"Tonight," she said with conviction. She explained that they were going on a date to a football game, and then over to a friend's house with a few other couples to make pizza and have a little get-together. It would be the perfect time to talk.

Michelle said good-bye and turned to leave. When she got to the door I said, "Michelle, at about 9:00 tonight, I'll say a little prayer for you." Her face lit up, a big smile appeared, and she went on her way.

When I saw her coming into class on Monday, I could already tell the weekend had been successful. Her face radiated happiness and victory.

After class she came up and said, "Want to hear about one of the most difficult and yet most wonderful times of my life?" I was eager to hear, and she told me the whole story.

Michelle and her boyfriend went on their date to the football game. He wasn't playing because of an injury so they left early. They went over to the girl's house where the party was to be held. No one else was there yet. They went around to the backyard and lay down on the lawn "to look at the stars."

To even lay down next to each other did not feel right to Michelle anymore. Almost immediately her boyfriend began their usual pattern of intimacy, but this time Michelle sat up and said, "No more, Ron. I'm not going to do that anymore."

"What do you mean," said Ron, somewhat startled. "You're my girl, and the evidences of your love for me is that privilege."

"Not anymore," Michelle replied firmly.

"Are you saying I don't have that right anymore?" asked Ron.

"That's right. It's all over."

"I told you if you don't let me, you don't love me. So I guess that's that. So long Michelle." With that, he got up and walked away.

"What did you do?" I asked Michelle.

"I sat there and cried," she said. "I didn't want to lose him. I love him. But I knew my decision was right, and it was what I really wanted to do. If we had continued, I wouldn't have had him anyway—eternally." I was so proud of her.

After she regained her composure, she went into the house and joined some of the other girls in the kitchen making pizza. Then she noticed the boys sitting together in the den. Ron was with them, but actually sitting alone. His hand was over his eyes and his head was slightly bowed.

She went into the room and put her hand tenderly on his shoulder to comfort him. He suddenly looked up at her. "And do you know what?" Michelle asked, "He had tears in his eyes, Brother Black. That great big, rough-and-tough football player had tears in his eyes."

Ron got up, took her by the hand, and walked her outside. He turned her around, placed his hands on her shoulders, and in a shaky voice said, "Thank God for you, Michelle. Thank you for finally doing what I wanted to do, but couldn't. Please forgive me. Love me. Don't leave me. I need you—on your grounds."

Those sweet, beautiful kids put their lives together again. They made appointments with their bishops, and went through the steps of repentance that were outlined.

Well, time passes doesn't it? And time passed for Ron and Michelle. One day several months later, I was walking on the BYU campus when I heard someone call, "Brother Black, wait a moment."

I looked around and there was my friend, Michelle. She looked so good—spiritually healthy and happy. We talked, and I asked if there was a special young man in her life. She responded with a nod in the affirmative. I asked if I knew him. "It's Ron!" she said, and told me he was on his mission. I beamed with approval.

She said everything was fine, except that he signed his name "Elder." I smiled with added approval and said, "Oh, that's a good sign, Michelle. He's not only in love with you, but also with the Lord and the mission."

More time passed, and I received one of those triple-folded announcements with a little sticker on the back. It indicated that Ron and Michelle requested the pleasure of our company at their marriage ceremony to be held in the House of the Lord.

My mind wandered back to that special day in seminary, and I reflected on the strength and courage of this young daughter of our Heavenly Father. Her desire to do right had literally turned two lives away from the paths of unhappiness and sin, and toward the path of righteousness and joy.

There is unmistakable power in righteous womanhood.

Chapter Four

Ask of God in All Things

*"Search diligently, pray always, and be believing, and all things shall work together for your good. . . ." * (D&C 90:24)

Again and again, we are told in sacred records that in order to enter the Kingdom of God we need to become like little children. That kind of total faith and love is a definite prerequisite. But sometimes when seemingly small circumstances arise, I mistakenly feel I can handle them on my own, without divine influence or inspiration. On one particular occasion, I found myself wondering how our Father in Heaven could possibly help with this situation. It was the beginning of a cold, wintery day, and I had to be at the airport by 7:00 a.m. I had left home at 5:30 to get there, but about halfway to the airport the car began to swerve unexpectedly. The thought that it could be a flat tire came to mind, coupled with the hope that I was wrong. Unfortunately, the tire was flat.

I got the car stopped and pulled over to the far right next to the guardrail. There was no available shoulder safely off the freeway, and this did not add any pleasure to the displeasure I was already feeling.

That early in the morning it was still dark, and I left the flashing lights on as I got out of the car and went around to the trunk. I found the little jack stand and the main assembly, but couldn't find the combination jack handle and lug wrench. I did find a star variety lug wrench, but to my great dismay, it would not fit into the jack-raising mechanism. I began to search the trunk more intently.

It was only then I remembered I had removed the tool to use on another vehicle and neglected to replace it. What could I do? I found a little bar of light metal in the trunk and attempted to utilize it as the handle, but to no avail.

To add insult to injury, it started to rain. I turned on the headlights and began looking around the front of the car for anything that would make do for the job. There was nothing. The rain changed to light snow, and I began to get worried. I feared missing my plane. The thought of prayer came to mind but was accompanied with feelings of doubt. "What could Heavenly Father actually do?" I thought. The cars that passed did so at a high rate of speed. I was at a place in the road where it was extremely difficult to see my car until right upon it. Because of this, it would have been difficult for another car to stop and help. My situation was dangerous as well.

I began walking back down the freeway, hoping I would find something to use as a jack handle. In the darkness, however, it was useless. I began to worry more about the time passing. Missing that particular flight would mean missing my speaking assignment that evening. It was a complicated travel schedule and had to be followed exactly for everything to work out.

The thought that I should pray recurred. Finally, I paused by the side of the road, bowed my head, and while the soft, white flakes of snow settled on and around me I asked the Lord for help.

After praying, I felt new hope and began walking down the dark freeway. I reasoned that as the oncoming cars passed me, their headlights would expose a section of the freeway and allow me to continue searching for something to use as a jack handle. For nearly a quarter of a mile I didn't see anything. I felt I should cross over to the other side of the guardrail, and as I did I noticed the stump of an older section of the rail.

I knew the railing itself was attached with long, steel bolts with washers, and I felt the post in the dark. To my excitement such a bolt was still in its original hole, even though the railing metal was long gone. My mind soared with the hope that there would not be an attached washer and nut.

I quickly reached behind the stump, and to my great disappointment felt the large, steel nut still securely fastened to the bolt. I knew the chances of unscrewing the nut were next to none, but I tried. I held onto the smooth carriage bolt-head as well as my wet and cold fingers could, said an emergency prayer, and made the first attempt. The nut turned. I told myself not to get too excited, as no doubt the nut would soon stop because of rust.

But it didn't stop. It came off as easily as a new nut comes off a new bolt. I was so ecstatic that I laughed out loud. I hopped over the guardrail and, with great exuberance thanked my Heavenly Father. As I neared the car and put the jack in place, the thought suddenly came to me, "What if the bolt is too big for the existing hole in the jacking assembly?" I took the bolt, and with near inability because of nervousness and the cold, attempted to slip it into the hole. It fit perfectly.

Again, however, doubt entered my mind. "What if the bolt bends as you jack it?" I thought. But the bolt didn't bend. It was *the* replacement tool for the job.

Soon, I was on my way again, a bit dirty, wet, cold, and tired, but on my way. I made it to the airport with just enough time, counting my run from the parking lot to the ticket counter. I thanked my Heavenly Father many times that day for the blessed principle of prayer, the very lifeline between us. What would our lives be without it? How lonely. How risky. Our Heavenly Father is there for us and He wants to help—even with the small, everyday things.

A Prayer Before Signing

My wife and I were in the process of selling our home. We hoped to use the proceeds toward the purchase of a larger home. A fair offer had been made, but we still had doubts. As the real estate agent presented us with the papers to review and sign, Ann caught my attention and motioned for us to leave the room for a moment. We excused ourselves and went into an adjoining room.

Ann asked me how I felt about the offer, and I told her I felt fairly good about it, though I wasn't completely sure we should take it. She then suggested we have a word of prayer about the matter. We stood there and uttered a short prayer, expressing our desire for inspiration and help in making this decision. Following the prayer, we felt better and were excited to accept the offer and sign the necessary papers.

We then immediately pursued plans to build a new home. But, much to our surprise, when we offered the prepared plans to the lending institution, we were told in a nice but firm way that we were financially unqualified to buy such a home. We left with deflated spirits and returned to the small apartment where we were living and wondered if our stay there was going to be more permanent than we had expected.

One day, shortly after, Ann's father mentioned he'd learned of some land for sale. The land seemed to be priced fairly and in a good location. We looked it over and decided to purchase the land for future building plans, when we were better qualified. As we later reviewed the entire transaction, we realized it would not have been possible to purchase the land had we not recently sold our home. We also realized the turn of events as an answer to our "emergency prayer" just before signing. It had been the right time to sell that house, and the decision was a sound one.

But why had the lending institution turned down our plans for building? That still troubled us, and we decided to try it again.

About two months after the first attempt, we thoroughly discussed the matter, then took the same plans to a different lending institution. We did not want to find ourselves with "too much month left over at the end of the money," but we did hope to build a home. After carefully reviewing our loan application, the loan officer informed us he saw no reason we couldn't continue with our plans to build the home just as we had originally hoped to.

We were pleasantly surprised. Still, we wondered about the hesitancy of the first loan officer. As we made arrangements and continued in prayer, we came to an interesting realization. At the time we approached the first loan company, the current rate of interest was fairly high. But by enduring the mysterious and unexpected delay, interest rates had dropped nearly 2 percent. Not only could we now afford the home we desired, but we were even able to add an additional room. We quickly located a suitable builder and began negotiations with him. One month after signing with the contractor, there was a blanket increase in construction costs, and the base price of all buildings rose many hundreds of dollars. We were within the lower rate by one month.

Looking over the entire experience, we recognized the tremendous influence our Heavenly Father has in our lives if we really believe in His ability to bless and care in all things.

The words of the Lord to the Prophet Joseph Smith are true: "But ye are commanded in all things to ask of God, who giveth liberally; and that which the Spirit testifies unto you even so I would that ye should do in all holiness of heart . . . doing all things with prayer and thanksgiving . . . " (D&C 46:7).

"AND BLESS HER PARENTS TO UNDERSTAND"

She had been out all night, and the following day someone told her to go over to the seminary. She looked tired, was obviously unhappy, and wanted help. At age fourteen she had already experimented with drugs and immorality.

When she arrived at my office, we discussed the events of her life. She was dissatisfied with herself and wanted freedom from the bad choices she had already made. I tried to help her understand who she was and the worth of her soul. I reminded her of her responsibility as a daughter of God, and told her that He was most likely disappointed with her behavior. During the conversation she informed me she was of another faith, but she listened intently to all I said.

At the conclusion of our talk, she told me she was afraid to go home. She feared her father would beat her—as he had before. I asked if she would like to kneel in prayer with me, that together we might call upon our Father in Heaven for His comfort and intervention in the matter. She told me again that she belonged to another faith, and I carefully explained our belief in God and Christ and the great importance of prayer. I told her the steps involved in prayer, and she readily accepted them. We knelt together on a small remnant of carpeting I secretly called my "prayer rug." Students from past seminary classes had recommended it for kneeling on the hard floor while praying.

During our prayer, I asked the Lord to comfort this young lady's body and spirit that she would feel good again. I prayed that He would help her overcome her weaknesses. At the close of the prayer I felt prompted to ask a special blessing upon her parents, that they would readily, lovingly, and understandingly accept her upon her return home. We arose, both feeling very good about the experience, and my young friend left the office to return home.

I received a phone call at home that night but was not there to talk to the caller. She said she would call back. The following morning at the office the phone rang, and it was the same woman, the girl's mother. She asked if I was the one who had talked with her daughter the day before. I felt a little reluctant to answer, assuming she was upset about the counseling and prayer.

"Yes," I said almost apologetically. "I talked with your daughter yesterday."

"Well," she said, "my husband and I would like to thank you for helping and encouraging our daughter to come home to us yesterday. We were so thrilled when she arrived. Thank you."

After we had talked, I hung up the phone, and bowed my head in prayer once again. And this time the words were of gratitude and thankfulness.

BLESSING ON THE TREES

One early morning my wife and I received a phone call from a lady across town. The woman was aware of the fact that we loved trees, and she had three beautiful pine trees in her backyard that she had to take out because of a renovation project. She asked if we would be interested in having the trees. I told her we would be over soon to look at them to see if it would be possible to remove the trees successfully.

I rounded up a couple of neighbors, and we headed across town. The trees were beautiful. We decided we would try to remove them, and the excavation project began. The more we dug, the bigger the job became. There were a lot of roots to one of those trees. We dug for three hours, and none of the pines would give up the security of its position.

In desperation, we finally attached a long rope to the base of each tree and attached the other end to my neighbor's four-wheel-drive pickup. He got in, gave it a little extra power, and out the trees came, one after the other. We got our trees, but there had been some serious sounds and snaps. We were afraid they wouldn't survive the transplantation.

We filled the truck with the three trees and hurriedly drove back to our neighborhood. My neighbor's big yard across the street was the obvious place for the largest and most beautiful of the trees. We dug a large hole and slid the gorgeous plant off the truck and into its new home.

The next was the smallest tree. The neighbor to our right wanted that one. We dug another hole, and replanted the small tree. We then dug the third hole in our backyard and planted the last tree. The trees looked beautiful in our yards, and we were proud of our work.

Early the next morning, I went to inspect our newly acquired forest friend, but things didn't look good. All the tiny tips of new growth were turned down, and my heart went the same direction. I was so disappointed.

My mind searched for possible solutions. Suddenly, I remembered Amulek's discourse on prayer. In it, he specifically says we should pray for our families, flocks and crops (see Alma 34:24-25). I knew that Amulek would not have said this if it were not true. I also knew that the prophet Mormon would not have left it in the abridgment if it were not true and good. This was my answer.

Just as I was looking for a quiet, obscure place to kneel, my oldest son came by. I explained the circumstance and asked if he would like to pray with me. We knelt together and I offered the prayer, asking our Father in Heaven to strengthen this young tree and the others we had transplanted.

When we stood, I glanced at the tips of the branches to see if there had been any immediate change. Not yet. But out of the corner of my eye, I did see something else. I saw a young man standing at the other side of our yard, watching us. A feeling of embarrassment came over me. It was such a personal matter.

"Hi, Al. How are you doing?" I said weakly.

He answered me and then asked pointedly, "What were you doing over there?" There was no way out. I tried to think of a tactful way to tell this young man of another faith that we were praying for the trees. My son jumped over a nearby fence and was gone. I was left alone to explain.

"Well, Al," I said, "we have a set of scriptures in our Church we refer to as the Book of Mormon. You've heard of it haven't you?" Al nodded. "Well," I said, "in that book, one of the early prophets encouraged the people to pray about anything they needed help with, including their crops and flocks. I believe what he said and we were just praying that our new pine tree would gain back its strength. It doesn't look too good, does it?"

Al stood there with a puzzled look on his face. "Oh!" he said, and slowly walked away, apparently wondering about these Mormons and what he had just heard.

By the end of the day, the tree was not doing any better. The ends of the branches hung lifelessly low, and I was disappointed. Deciding that the tree might like a cool shower of water, I grabbed the hose, turned on the water, and sprayed it all over. Still no change.

About this time, dark storm clouds began to close in overhead. The wind came up and brought with it a torrent of rain. It was as if Heavenly Father said, "Move over my son. Let me show you how to water that tree." The pine's branches were soaked deeply within, and the ground drank up the rain. In our prayers that night we again mentioned our desire for the trees to live.

In the morning, I rushed outside to inspect the tree, and to my great joy, those new, green shoots of life were pointing in a healthy upward direction. To someone else, it might not have been anything noteworthy, but to us the tree's improvement was a tiny yet significant miracle.

This story doesn't end here. Months later, I received a phone call. A young, enthusiastic voice said, "Hi, Don. How would you like to come to my baptism next Saturday?"

"Who is this?" I asked.

The friendly voice said, "Al."

I assured him we would be thrilled to be present at this momentous occasion.

The appointed hour came, and we took our places with the others in the audience. Following the sacred ordinance, Al was asked to share his testimony with his friends. He stood and related his feelings about baptism, and then told us how he became interested in the church.

"There is a fellow in the audience that did something that made me think very seriously about this wonderful church," said Al. "I caught him one day in the very act of praying for a sick pine tree in his backyard. I thought anyone who believed such things had to have something in his faith and church teachings that other people don't have, and I wanted to know more about it. That event impressed me and affected my beliefs, and led me to investigate the church."

My heart swelled with warmth and thanksgiving for the words of a prophet and for the great principle of prayer.

A Scholarship, the Temple, and the Lord

Together with the other teachers of the seminary, I was to arrange for the graduation exercises in our stake. One of our assignments was to submit to the stake presidency a list of those students we thought might be worthy of a significant scholarship to BYU. I gathered a list of names from the seminary teachers who had students in that stake and submitted the list to the stake president.

A day or two later the list was back on my desk with a note attached, asking me to narrow down the number of prospective candidates. I took the list, looked it over, and suddenly felt wrong about most of the names I had previously felt right about. Four or five new names came to mind and I wrote them down. I was also asked to show a sequential preference regarding the candidates. I put a numerical value next to the appropriate names, and the list was submitted again to the stake president.

No more was mentioned about the scholarship until the evening of seminary graduation when the winner was to be announced. An envelope containing the winner's name was handed to the first counselor and he opened it. There was a hush over the audience as everyone anticipated someone's thrilling next moment. The name was read, and a cry was heard from one of the young ladies in the graduating group. She came forward and with tears flowing down her cheeks, graciously accepted her award. What a wonderful surprise for her!

Following the ceremony, the young lady's parents came up and asked me if I had known who the winning student was prior to the announcement. I told them I had not, although the list of names was handled through me. I also explained how difficult it was to choose the final candidates, and that the final list of names had even been revised to include students who hadn't been listed previously. I then mentioned that the number one had been placed by their daughter's name almost as an afterthought.

They asked me to repeat what I had just said. I did, and they asked when all of this had taken place. Tears welled up in their eyes when I told them the day. I sensed they were feeling something special and asked them to share it with me.

The story they told was one of the nicest answers to prayer I had ever heard. The young lady who had won the scholarship was their oldest daughter. She wanted to attend college, but coming from a large family the chances were slim that her parents could meet the additional expenses. They didn't know what the answer was, but decided to go to the temple to seek greater spiritual guidance.

In the temple these faithful parents sought help through prayer. It was on the same day that the strong urge came over me to change the original names on the scholarship list and to put the number one before their daughter's name.

Discovering the full details of this event brought a stronger conviction to me of the greatness of our gospel, and gave strength to Alma's words: "Yea, and cry unto God for all thy support; yea . . . counsel with the Lord in all thy doings" (Alma 37:36-37). Isn't it wonderful that the Lord hears our prayers and takes time to influence and direct our lives.

THE PLAN OF SALVATION—
WITH AND WITHOUT THE SPIRIT

To me, prayer is the backbone of a relationship between God and His children. It is latent power at our command, a talk between our Heavenly Father and ourselves.

As a missionary I had an experience that reinforced my personal testimony of the power that comes through prayer and teaching by the Spirit.

Sister Petersen had embraced the gospel. She felt deeply the added dimension the gospel message had given her life, and though her husband had long ago rejected the entire idea, she desired to share the gospel with her daughter.

It was necessary to meet with Sister Peterson and her sixteen-year-old daughter at the chapel because her husband would not even tolerate the presence of the elders in his home. The daughter was an intelligent young lady and enjoyed learning the various aspects of the gospel. At the close of each discussion, she was clearly interested in knowing more. At last we had the opportunity to teach her about the plan of salvation.

On the day of our appointment to present this message, I received a new missionary as a companion. He was nineteen years old. This was in the days prior to the intense language training that takes place now, and everyone was a bright shade of green when they arrived in the mission field. We walked from our apartment across the street to the chapel and met Sister Petersen and her daughter.

I was a veteran missionary, and would be leaving for home in just three months. Unfortunately, a little overconfidence had found its way into my life at this time, and I neglected to have prayer before we left for the appointment. "Oh, well," I reasoned, "I know this lesson well enough."

We sat around a table and began the lesson. Mechanically I whizzed through the entire plan. Our young investigator sat patiently without much involvement while I "threw" point after point of good, heavy doctrine at her. When I had finished, I turned to her and confidently said, "Well, that's the great plan of salvation. What do you think?"

She looked up from her fixed position and softly said, "I feel sorry for you. Do you really believe all that?"

I had never felt such a sharp, piercing blow to my spirit. "What do you mean?" I asked. "Isn't that a beautiful plan?"

She again softly replied, "How can anyone believe such things. Maybe I'm not interested in this religion after all."

I couldn't believe what was being said. This lesson had always been my strongest. I loved it. I felt it. My heart ached with disappointment.

My young companion, sitting there and fighting the boredom of not yet understanding the language, looked up and quietly said, "How's it going, Elder?" I responded with a facial expression of disappointment. The young lady was now obviously ready to end the meeting, and yet was kind enough to accept another appointment in two days. We had a closing prayer and departed.

Walking across the street to our apartment, my new companion asked innocently, "How'd it go, Elder?" What a thing to have to report to a new Elder, bubbling with faith.

After a few moments, I simply replied, "Not so good. We need to have an emergency session with our Heavenly Father, right now."

We knelt on the floor in our apartment to pray. I wanted to cry. I had disappointed my Heavenly Father and myself. It seemed I was standing alone, temporarily without the spirit. It was a terrible, lonesome feeling. It's strange how even "veterans" are kept in line.

I pleaded with the Lord to forgive me for trying to present such a holy message without Him. I begged Him for a change of spirit on behalf of our investigator. I felt deeply humbled, and as I prayed, I felt an answer to our sincere supplications. Completing the communication, we arose and I turned to my companion. "We have an appointment," I said.

"Now?" he asked.

"Now," I assured him.

We hopped on our bikes and sped through the streets of the city. Arriving at a large apartment complex, we hurriedly walked to the third floor. "Who is the appointment with?" my companion asked. I rang the bell and as the door opened, we looked into the face of the young lady we had just taught. My companion looked very confused, but it all made sense to me. This was the answer I had received to our prayer.

The young girl looked very surprised and excitedly asked why we were there. "We must tell you something about the gospel," I said. Suddenly she didn't look excited at all. I told her there was a very important part of the lesson I had left out, and asked if we could have another hour with her as soon as possible. She reminded me of our appointment in a couple of days, but I told her it had to be sooner. She asked when, and I said, "Right now!"

She agreed hesitantly, and soon we were again sitting around the same table at the chapel. But this time there was an important difference. My companion and I knelt humbly before our Father prior to entering that room, pleading for a second chance and the presence of the Spirit. I gave the very same lesson as before, but the Spirit was there and the difference it made was tangible. That day I learned the contrast between mechanical and spiritual presentation of the same subject.

Our young investigator sat quietly throughout the lesson, and tears occasionally filled her eyes. We all thrilled at the greatness of the beautiful and sacred plan of salvation. Upon completion of the presentation, I looked at the young lady and said, "What do you think of our Father's great plan of salvation?" Clearing her throat and wiping away tears, she sweetly replied, "Oh, it's magnificent. Why didn't you tell me about it before?"

Sitting there together, we basked in the sweet presence of the Spirit. We thanked our Father for His presence, and for allowing us the companionship of the Holy Ghost. And I thanked Him for the great and powerful gift of prayer.

No Room at This Inn–for Mormons!

It was the Saturday night before a district conference, and the missionaries of our district gathered together at the chapel. Saturday nights at conference time in Denmark were big affairs for us. The members host festivities and games, provide treats of every imaginable variety, and present a gala talent show.

Our mission president was in attendance. We were honored to have him with us because he was a man of great spirit and testimony, and we loved him. The missionaries were scattered throughout the audience waiting for the talent show to begin when we heard the announcement that our mission president was wanted on the phone.

In a few minutes word came back that all the elders were to meet in a nearby office with the president. When we had gathered, he stood before us and said, "Elders, your brothers in the gospel, Elders Sorensen and Jorgensen, are trying to open a very difficult area that fosters much hate and deep misunderstanding of our beliefs. They just called to tell me they cannot find a place to live, even though they've been trying most of this day. Will you join with me in prayer, and through our faith ask the Lord to help them with this problem? By the way, I told them they would find a place within the next half hour."

I remember the thrill that came over me as we knelt together as brothers holding the Melchizedek Priesthood. I could feel the power in the room. We knelt in a large circle and the mission president offered the prayer. There was a warm, lovely feeling present. Following the prayer, we again joined the Saints in the cultural hall. Later that evening, the president told us he received word that the elders had found a place to live within a half hour after our prayer, exactly as they were promised.

Prayer is our link with our Heavenly Father. He will answer us when we petition Him.

Chapter Five

Angels Above Us Are Silent Notes Videotaping

*"And the book which was the book of life is the
record which is kept in heaven . . ."*
(D&C 128:7)

Some years ago I was serving as a park ranger assistant in a nearby state park. I liked the work because it allowed me to be out of doors and work with people in a pleasant setting.

One day, while on duty at the main entrance to the park, my partner drove up in the ranger truck and relieved me for lunch. I jumped into the truck, drove slowly over to a small trailer we used as headquarters, and commenced to build myself a peanut butter and jam sandwich. Suddenly, I heard voices not far away. I leaned over to the little window of the trailer and pushed the curtain to one side so I could see out. Three young men were sitting on a nearby picnic bench, and I tried to see if any of them happened to have been seminary students of mine.

One of the boys *had* been in my class the previous semester. I was just about to rap on the window to get his attention when I noticed that two of the boys were cupping cigarettes behind their backs. They were sitting with their backs toward me and didn't realize I was there, or the view I had. They would lean back slightly and take a puff, then sit forward again and cleverly cup the cigarettes behind them. I didn't know who they were hiding them from. Certainly not me.

I leaned forward against the window to see more clearly. There in the river some fifty feet in front of them were a couple of young ladies attempting to drive one of those pontoon outfits you steer and pedal.

When the girls got just about in front of where the boys were they suddenly "lost control" and were unable to steer. Round and round they went in front of their admiring audience.

The boys took the bait and began calling encouragement to the girls. However, in low voices they thought no one could hear, they began making highly inappropriate comments, and these comments continued for some time.

I sat at the window feeling a little like Heavenly Father must feel when He sees and hears that sort of activity from His children. The boys had no idea that a seminary teacher was within fifteen feet of them. The words of the song, "Do What Is Right," came to mind, particularly the part where the lyrics read, "Angels above us are silent notes taking." A latter-day "Inspired Version" came to mind—"Angels above us are silent notes videotaping."

I thought about the fact that every time we do wrong our actions are instantly recorded in the eyes of unseen beholders and in our book of life.

The time came to return to my post. I hated to embarrass the boys, but I had to leave. I cocked my "Smokey the Bear" hat to one side to help conceal my identity, and stepped outside.

But my disguise didn't work. I heard one boy suddenly say, "Did you see who that was?"

"Oh, no!" another voice said. "Do you think he saw us?"

The third voice chimed in, "Sure he did, stupid!"

I wanted so badly to stop and say, "Yes, I did see you! But not only did I see you, but your Heavenly Father saw you, too." I didn't say anything to the boys. I hoped a lesson was taught just in the embarrassment they felt.

I contemplated that incident long afterward. Often others are watching us when we least expect it, or know it.

Not long after the first incident took place, I had the opportunity to be an unseen observer again.

CHALLENGES IN THE NIGHT

I was walking home from a late meeting at church. It was Christmas time, and, as I walked, I passed a small shopping center. Everything was colorful and festive, and I paused momentarily to enjoy the decorated display windows.

While standing there, I heard voices from the nearby street, and in a moment three teenage boys appeared under the streetlight to my left. As always, I looked carefully to see if I knew any of them. Two of the boys looked familiar, and one of them was a seminary student of mine.

As had happened before, I was just about to call out his name in greeting, when I noticed one of the boys pull a can of beer from the pocket of his large army coat.

The unfolding drama became tense as the boy opened the can and took a big swallow. He then handed the can to his impatient friend, who also took a big drink. When the second boy was finished, he handed the can to the young man in my class.

My seminary-teacher intuition was to yell out, "Don't do it!" But I thought of the shock of an unexpected voice suddenly coming out of the dark night and decided this was a test he must face on his own. I watched with great anticipation. The beads of moisture on the beer can somewhat matched those on this boy's brow. Seconds that seemed like minutes passed. "Hurry! We want it back," the boys said impatiently. My student grasped the can, looked at it, and finally said, "Here, I don't want any," and handed the can back to the first boy.

I was so happy and proud of my young friend, I wanted to shout out, "Nice going!" But, again, I thought of how such a shout might go over in the dark when they thought they were all alone.

As I walked the rest of the way home, I reviewed that incident again and again in my mind. Little do we know when it will be our turn to be tested and who may be watching our actions.

Let It Shine

As a young boy, I attended a memorial service in honor of those who gave their all for the victory of World War II. It was held in the Los Angeles coliseum, and upon entering that huge edifice each person was given a small book of matches.

During the memorial service, there was an impressive display of military might. We saw jeeps, tanks, trucks, and troops. There was even a model version of the famous "Fighting Lady" aircraft carrier, built on the trailer unit of a diesel truck.

At the conclusion of the service, the voice of the announcer came over the public-address system. "Ladies and gentlemen," he said, "upon entering the coliseum this evening you received a small packet of matches. Would you take them out now? We are going to dim the spotlights overhead. Upon the count of three, would you all kindly light one match in honor of those who died for freedom's sake."

The lights dimmed, and we heard the count, "one-two-three." At that moment, everyone who could, lit one little match. The entire coliseum was illuminated in unbelievable brightness.

Many years later, I heard something that brought that memorial service to mind. I was sitting in a small room in the newly constructed London Temple in Newchapel, England. We had gathered to witness the dedicatory service and prayer of that holy building, and the prophet, David O. McKay, was in our midst.

Prior to the dedicatory prayer, President McKay spoke to the members of the church. Among other things he said, "Brothers and Sisters, let your little lights shine brightly in this naughty world." At first, the magnitude of this inspired statement and admonition didn't fully register with me. However, as I thought it over later, my mind went back to that impressive experience in the open arena of the Los Angeles Coliseum. I saw the thousands of flickering lights dissipate the darkness, and suddenly I understood the great importance of President McKay's words. What a message for each member of the Church!

I thought of the power of one little light—the power of one member, faithfully doing what is right and allowing the light of truth to shine brightly for all to see. There is a special power in righteous example, and we each have a light that the world desperately needs to see. Let it shine!

ONE LITTLE LIGHT

There was once a boy in the church who found himself in the "no-name" category. The boy just didn't fit into any particular group. His mind did not qualify him for intellectual debate activities, his confidence was lacking for school government, and although he felt he could have excelled in track, no one encouraged him in that direction.

His self-esteem dropped to a dangerously low point. He began to think that to be accepted by any group would be better than being alone, even if it meant lowering his standards.

After awhile, the young man noticed that the only students who seemed to want him as a friend comprised the so-called "hood" element of the school, but acceptance of any kind was better than nothing. Besides, in his school at that time there were gang fights and constant threats of reprisals among different ethnic groups. There was safety in numbers—especially if you were numbered among the tough group.

One day, about midway through his senior year of high school, his parents told him they were going to move to another home thirty-five miles away. The boy put up a terrible fight and refused to leave his school and buddies. They verbally had it out, with the result being a compromise. He was permitted to stay with his sister and brother-in-law until graduation. It was a bad solution in a sense, for as good as his sister was, she was not that much older than the boy. She had no experience with supervising teenagers.

The young man began to keep late hours and the situation grew worse. One night he came in with his lips swollen and his teeth loose—the result of being attacked by a drunken boy at a party. He left another party just before someone fired a rifle at a rival gang and hit a girl in the chest. Clearly, Satan and his henchmen were closing in.

School was finally over, and the boy graduated and moved back in with his parents in their new home. An alert bishop became aware of his return and called four young ladies in the ward. He told the girls about the boy and asked if they would be willing to help him find his way back to the church. The girls agreed to help, and the next Sunday they went to his home.

This young man was used to sleeping in on Sundays, and he was not happy with the disturbance. He asked what they wanted, and they invited him to go to church with them. He thanked them in a sarcastic tone and told them he wasn't interested. They left, and he went back to bed.

The following Sunday they returned. Once again they woke him up and once again he refused to attend church. They left, and he went back to bed.

On the third Sunday he was shocked. They were back again. Where did they find the courage to keep coming, he wondered. "Wait a minute," he told them. "I'll make you a deal. If you promise not to come back to my house, I'll come to one of your meetings." The girls agreed, and it was decided he would attend MIA on Wednesday.

Wednesday evening came. Intentionally the young man arrived late. Everyone was going into the cultural hall for a roadshow rehearsal, but he stood outside in the patio area of the building. The doors were open, and he could see the activities inside. Suddenly, he saw a girl standing in the crowded room somewhat apart from the others. She stood under a spotlight in the ceiling and her golden hair seemed to shine. He liked what he saw.

Two boys in the ward walked past him, and he stopped them to ask, "Who's that girl over there?" The boys turned to look, and then one answered, "Oh, that's Deann Tibbetts. She's one of the girls in the ward."

"Is she going with anybody?" the young man asked.

"No," they said. "Not really."

The young man walked into the crowded room, and over to where the pretty girl stood. He said hello, and she cautiously returned the greeting. What she didn't do was whip out her mini-scriptures and say, "You know what Paul says about your long hair." In no way did she make him feel uncomfortable.

They began to talk and discovered that their parents knew each other. This was a tiny toehold for continued conversation until the young man could gather his courage. Finally he just blurted out the words, "Would you like to go out with me?"

It is likely the girl wanted to decline, but instead she answered, "Yes, I think that would be nice."

"How about Friday night?" he asked.

"I can't go Friday night," she said. "How about Sunday afternoon?"

"I didn't think you could date on Sundays."

"Oh, sure," she said. "A lot has probably happened since you've been to church."

"Okay," he said. "Let's go bowling on Sunday."

"No," she said kindly. "Let's go to church."

"Church!" he exclaimed. "That ain't no date."

"Well," she said sweetly, "take it, or leave it."

"I'll take it," he said.

They went to church the following Sunday afternoon. Those who spoke had prepared their messages, and when the final speaker bore his testimony the Holy Ghost carried it across the room and into the heart of that young man. He felt an unfamiliar tingle all over his body, and he liked it, even though it was a bit embarrassing to someone trying to play a tough-guy role.

They returned the following Sunday, and the next. He began to attend Sunday School and Priesthood meetings, too. Then, one evening, when he and Deann were driving on a date, she turned toward him and said, "You know what you'd be?"

"No," he asked. "What?"

"A great elder in the Melchizedek Priesthood," she said sweetly.

"Not me," he said defiantly. "I don't know anything about that high stuff."

Not many months later, Deann joined the bishop and the young man's parents in the bishop's office as they conferred upon the young man the Melchizedek Priesthood and made him an elder. She silently rejoiced, as did they.

Time passed, and they were on another date together. Again Deann turned and watched him as he drove. "What are you looking at?" he asked.

"You!" she answered.

"Why?"

"Oh, I was just thinking about something."

"What?" he asked.

"Oh, what you'd be good as," she said.

He thought a moment, then replied, "Don't say it."

She did anyway. "You'd be a great missionary."

"I don't know anything about the gospel," he said.

A few months later, Deann sat on the front row of the chapel as that same young man attempted to give the second talk of his life. It was his farewell address prior to leaving to go halfway around the world to serve as a missionary for the Church of Jesus Christ in the country of Denmark.

Those two and a half years changed this young man's life, and the lives of many others. Isn't that a great story? I particularly like it, because I was that young man. To this day I thank a loving, caring and sensitive Heavenly Father for Deann Tibbetts and others like her who played such an important role in my life.

No, I didn't marry Deann, but she helped me arrange my life to qualify for the one who would later become my wife. Deann was one Mormon girl who allowed her light to shine brightly, and it affected those around her. From Deann, I learned the power of a good example, and the ability of one who is living righteously to participate in the miracle of changing lives.

Chapter Six

Childlike Faith and Tiny Miracles

"Suffer the little children to come unto me, and forbid them not: for of such is the kingdom of God. Verily I say unto you, whoso-ever shall not receive the kingdom of God as a little child, he shall not enter therein. And he took them up in his arms, put his hands upon them, and blessed them." (MARK 10:14-16)

One day the members of our stake were asked if they could find in their hearts and pocketbooks the desire and ability to begin construction for our new stake center. The same challenge was given to the young people in our families. Little ones up to twelve years old were asked if they would give twenty-five dollars each. Teenagers were assessed seventy-five dollars.

We came home and explained to our five-year-old son what the Lord expected of us as members of the church in this area. We explained that this was a personal and rare opportunity to help contribute to the actual construction and creation of a beautiful new building. We felt it would be something we would always be able to enjoy and be proud of, now as well as in the future.

We asked our son if he would like to earn his own money to contribute to the building fund. With a great big smile and a tiny burst of enthusiasm, he made his answer apparent. As we look back in retrospect, it seems a little miracle was forming during those exciting times around our house.

One day soon after, a close friend came by and announced the opportunity to purchase end-of-season cases of candy from a closing resort spot nearby. It seemed the very way was opening for our son to earn his own contribution money for this new building. We bought two cases of the miscellaneous candy at a fraction of the original cost. We were learning once again the sweet, quiet principle of committing oneself to a cause and then witnessing the way opening to achieve it. With an assortment of candies neatly displayed in a red wagon and a handmade sign in place, off the little merchant went down the street. He knocked upon door after door, announcing to everyone that he was selling candy to "help build Heavenly Father's house!"

The special spirit of sacrifice and contribution that was felt throughout the stake was also being felt by one little five-year-old boy. Nearly every house in the neighborhood opened their doors and purchased from the vendor for Heavenly Father. With the additional effort of collecting pop bottles from neighbors and selling mistletoe, personally gathered from giant oak trees on a visit with family in California, the little savings soon swelled to a full twenty-five dollars. One little boy, with a borrowed wagon and a spirit to match the occasion, fulfilled his goal. He proudly handed the bishop an envelope containing his assessed amount.

Now the building is finished. It is a tribute to the sacrifice, love, and dedication of the members, and a very special reminder of one little boy's obedience and desire to please Heavenly Father.

DADDY, ARE YOU READY?

I was traveling to a speaking assignment. My wife and little son were with me, and we were crossing the mountains of the California high desert country. Having lived in southern California most of my growing years, I hadn't realized what a concern snowy weather could be when traveling, but soon found out! We were suddenly bombarded with snow that was driven by cold, heavy winds. The stretch of highway we were driving led up a steep mountain pass, and it was becoming very icy. Car by car began to slide, spin their tires, and pull over to the side. Trucks even began to lose traction and pull over.

I could feel our wheels beginning to spin on the steep grade, but I thought we might make it if we could maintain our speed. We swerved around the last, slowing cars, passing them precariously, and losing speed. I said fearfully, "I don't think we're going to make it, sweetheart. It doesn't look good." There was thoughtful silence from our usually noisy son, and I looked around for a moment to see if everything was all right back there. There he stood, between the front and back seat, his little arms folded, his eyes open wide, taking the whole matter into his little heart and mind. The silence was broken with his reply. He said sweetly, "I know how we can make it, Daddy."

I replied, "How, my son?"

He said, "Let's have a prayow!" (He was not able to properly enunciate his R's at this time). I said, "That's a great idea!" Dependent upon his sweet, childlike faith, I said, "Would you like to offer it?" He said, "Sho! Daddy, are you weddy?" I said, "Yes, I am." Then he began. "Heavenly Fathow. Pweese bwess us dat we won't cwash. In the name of Jesus Cwist, Amen."

Then he said, "You know why the prayow was so shote?" I said, "No, Why?" He said, "'Cuz I didn't want you to keep yo eyes closed too long!" In a moment or two I wiped the forming tears from them. We made it over the icy grade to my awaiting appointment. This special moment with our son, and the added safety we enjoyed because of his prayer, made it a blessed experience.

And Help Mommy and Daddy to be Happy

Some time ago, when the children were quite small, Ann and I found ourselves in a heated discussion that promised to lead to unkindness and provocation. We let things go too far, and didn't bridle our angry feelings. The spirit in the home began to deteriorate. We could sense that, but we didn't think the children would be able to.

After our main bout, time passed in near silence. Soon it was time for family prayer. Because neither Ann nor I were in the proper spirit to offer the prayer, I called upon our oldest son, then about six years old, to give it. He readily accepted the invitation, and I had the feeling he'd hoped he would be called upon.

We were kneeling together that evening as a somewhat unhappy family, and Tosh began speaking with his Heavenly Father in the typically direct way children approach prayer. After he'd said a few things such as "Bless that no bank robbers will come in our house tonight," and "Bless that no harms will bite us," he paused, and then his little voice continued, "and help Mommy and Daddy to be happy and to be friends again."

Ann's hand found mine, and warmth and love reentered the room. Pride vanished, and the needed, welcome, sweet family spirit returned. My heart uttered a silent song of joy for the blessing of little ones in our lives.

The words, "yea, even babes did open their mouths and utter marvelous things" (3 Nephi 26:16), filled my soul. Later, when the children had gone to bed and all was quiet and still, Ann and I thanked our Father in Heaven for this special blessing.

A Child's Faith in the Desert

We had left the city of Kermit, Texas, an hour previously, and were heading toward Carlsbad Caverns in the state of New Mexico. Already, it was time to stop, pull off the engine cover, and pull out number four spark plug to clean it—again. Our truck was not doing well. In fact, about every hundred miles it was necessary to perform this little plug ceremony just to keep the engine going.

Finishing the task and closing the engine cover, I placed the key into the ignition switch, turned it, and found no response. It had played this little game before, but a little fiddling with the key usually enticed it to make contact and turn over. Nothing happened this time. I tried repeatedly, but the engine did not turn over.

I got out of the truck, took a long screwdriver, and carefully nudged the open flywheel, which had made it start before. I tried the ignition again. Still no action. I repeated the process several more times, but with no success. I checked other wiring, but nothing made any difference, and I was getting worried. Time was passing, and I was out in the hot desert with two of my children.

Turning to them I said, "It doesn't look good, you guys. I guess whatever has been giving us trouble finally went out all the way. The engine won't even make a sound."

"What are we going to do, Daddy? I'm scared," my daughter said.

Suddenly, my son interrupted, "Don't be scared. Let's have a prayer. Heavenly Father will help us."

With my sometimes faithless adult mind, I thought, what could Heavenly Father possibly do to help us way out here in the desert without a town around for miles and miles either way?

Not wanting to disturb the sweet, childlike faith of a wonderful little son and his sweet sister, I said, "Well, okay, do you want to say it . . . please?" He responded with enthusiasm, "Sure, Dad!" He then began his sweet and simple prayer. As he said the words, "Heavenly Father, please help us with our truck way out here on the desert," I began to experience a tiny revelation.

The cause of the mechanical difficulty was absolutely and clearly defined in my mind, and I actually saw wires, a switch, and their location. Upon uttering an "amen" to his mighty, little prayer, I immediately began to take off the engine cover within the truck. I saw the wires that ran across the transmission to a little switch that was operated by the gear selector. I cut the wires, then spliced the two loose ends together, bypassing the switch. I replaced the engine cover, took my place behind the wheel, turned the key, and the engine faithfully started. Almost in one voice, we all said, "We better be sure to thank Heavenly Father for that one." We did, and I personally thanked him for the simple, unwavering faith of a child—the kind of faith that places total confidence and trust in a loving and ever-powerful Heavenly Father.

Chapter Seven

The Youth of Zion: Faithful and True

"True to the faith that our parents have cherished, true to the truth for which martyrs have perished. To God's command, soul, heart and hand, faithful and true we will ever stand." (FROM "SHALL THE YOUTH OF ZION FALTER" BY EVAN STEPHENS.)

Wendy's home has a country feeling. She loves horses and has her own. On a brisk but sunny day when Wendy was fifteen, she and her best girlfriend were out riding. Wendy had dismounted her horse to make an adjustment to her saddle and was preparing to mount again. She placed her left foot into the stirrup, preparatory to swinging herself up and onto the saddle. At the same moment, a woman motorist came speeding by, and without thinking, honked the horn as she passed.

Hearing the sudden blast of the horn, Wendy's horse reared, panicked, and went into a full gallop. Wendy couldn't remove her foot from the stirrup. Suddenly caught, and unable to grab the saddle to hoist herself up to a riding position, she found herself being dragged on the rough ground with no way to protect or support her body. About a half block later, the horse came to a halt. Wendy lay seriously injured, still hanging painfully from the stirrup. Her coat was torn in shreds, and her arms, back, and head were cut and bruised.

The woman who had honked, witnessed the tragedy, but drove on. Immediately Wendy felt a sharp pain in her leg. She could see it was broken. With the help of her girlfriend, she carefully climbed atop the horse and rode slowly the three miles to her home.

She was immediately rushed to the hospital, where it was determined that the injury was complex in nature, requiring surgery and a stainless steel screw in the broken leg to support the shattered bone structure. Following the usual preparation and anxiety of such an ordeal, Wendy went into surgery. She spent a few days at the hospital in recuperation, and then returned to her home to convalesce.

Days passed, and the pain persisted. As Wendy's seminary teacher, I went to visit her one evening. Her Father met me at the door to tell me Wendy wasn't feeling too well, but he was certain she would welcome my visit. I walked into her bedroom with her father and my heart suddenly ached. There lay this lovely girl, head turned to one side, with an expression of great pain and anguish. She was unaware of my presence, and cried aloud. Her hand tightly clutched the phone laying next to her.

Seeing her misery, I whispered to her father that maybe we shouldn't disturb her. She heard me and slowly turned her head. I quickly realized she was embarrassed to have her teacher see her bedridden and emotional. I walked to her side, took her hand, and said quietly, "How ya doin', Wendy? We sure miss you at school." She forced a slight smile to her face and said, "Not so good." She continued, showing the childlike faith the Savior so often referred to in the scriptures, and whispered, "Would you please bless me?"

I felt the maturity of her young spirit. Her faith was apparent. I graciously accepted the invitation, and her father was asked to participate also. We anointed and blessed Wendy. She lay still throughout the ordinance. When completed, she opened her eyes and quietly whispered, "The pain's gone now. Thank you." She then closed her eyes and fell into a restful sleep. God bless you, Wendy. Keep that sweet faith.

FULL-GROWN FAITH IN A SMALL BODY

I have often said I believe this generation of youth possesses an amazing ability to spring back from adversity. One young friend of mine exemplifies that kind of faith and resilience.

I first met Lanette when she was fifteen years old. She was an attractive girl with long blonde hair. She always seemed to be the very picture of springtime. There was a fresh, alive feeling about her. We became acquainted when her father and I participated on the same lecture tour.

Some time later, I heard that something had happened to Lanette. I wrote to find out more details, and in response received the following letter from her.

"Hello,

"Mom sent your letter to me (forwarded it) today. You see, I'm in the Elks Rehabilitation Center in Boise.

"You wanted to know about me. Well, here goes.

"The wreck happened on the first of October. I was doing dishes when two friends came and asked if I wanted to go driving around. Mom said she'd finish the dishes, so I went. That night a good movie was going to be on television, so about 5:00 p.m. we started home.

"We were driving on a narrow country road with deep ditches on both sides when we started to pass a car in front of us. Somehow we went down into the ditch on the left side of the road, came out of it and nearly hit the car ahead of us broadside. The driver spun the wheel and the back of the pickup we were driving bumped hard, went into the air, and blew a tire when it landed. We rolled seven times, finally ending up on the other side of the road in the ditch.

"The other two girls climbed out, but I was pinned in. All I could see was gray smoke, and I thought I was dead. However, I knew I was alive when I tried to breathe because you can't be dead and hurt like that. I didn't know it then, but my spinal cord had been severed between the seventh and eighth thoracic vertebrae. I'm paralyzed from the waist down, The doctors say I'll never walk again.

"I have to wear a brace on my back until the bones heal, but I should have it off by Christmas. There isn't much pain anymore. I'm progressing rapidly. Today I put on my own Levis and shoes and socks, all by myself, for the first time. It really made my day, even though it took me forty-five minutes.

"This accident has been the greatest thing that has ever happened to me. You see, I should have died, but I didn't. And I should be para- lyzed for the rest of my life, but I won't be. I figure two people can do anything, as long as one of them is God. I've put all the faith I have in God, and when it's time, I know I will walk. My faith grows more every day as I realize how much life has to offer. I'm too stubborn to stop living at sixteen.

"Every night in my prayers, I thank God for just being alive, and for still having my hands, eyes, mind, heart, and soul. The rest will come in time. Even if I never walk again, I have all eternity to run. I only hope I can be strong enough to live worthy of eternal life.

"I've got a lot of trials ahead of me, but I know there will be no miracle until the trial of my faith. I know God loves me and is watching out for me, and I have a conviction within myself that I'm going to make it. I don't say that to brag, quite the contrary. This experience has really humbled me. I'm so glad I know what I do. Some people search all their lives and never find the answers. I know. I'm sixteen, but I know, and I've got a beautiful life to live, if I will. I've seen here what happens to people when they give up. They die inside and that's much worse than physical death. I don't want to be like that. I won't!

"So don't say you're sorry this accident happened to me. I appreciate your concern, but it's been a blessing in my life. This might not make a lot of sense, but I think you understand how I feel.

"Well, that's about it for me. I've got a therapy session in ten minutes, so I better go.

"God be with you,

"Lanette."

I can't begin to express the impact Lanette's letter had on me. Her attitude about and understanding of the purpose of life were so far beyond her years. Certainly the song that compliments the "youth of the noble birthright" was meant for her. Her love of life, her faith, and her zeal continue to inspire me to stay in the race and do my best so one day I will be able to keep up with her. She will run again! Those youth of the noble birthright who are faithful and true will ever stand, walk, and run!

Chapter Eight

Help and Guidance, Liahona-Style

*"And it did work for them according to their faith in God;
therefore, if they had faith to believe that God could cause that those
spindles should point the way they should go, behold, it was done;
therefore they had this miracle, and also many other miracles
wrought by the power of God, day by day." (ALMA 37:40)*

When I read some of the revelations and information concerning the guidance of the Lord, and his interventions in mysterious ways on behalf of his children, I am amazed at how much we take for granted. There have been some experiences in my life that seem more than coincidental and which make me believe that we all have a personal Liahona if we but exercise the proper faith. One such incident will live in my memory for a long time to come. When I look back upon all the detailed circumstances surrounding this incredible experience, I marvel at the interest of the Lord in helping us overcome obstacles and do His work.

My assignment for the week was to speak at a youth conference on beautiful Catalina Island off the southern California coastline. I had figured out my agenda down to the minute to assure the scheduled arrival time. It would be necessary for me to leave that Friday afternoon directly following my sixth and last period of teaching. When the 3:00 bell rang, I ran for my briefcase, pulled the office door shut, and headed for the faculty parking lot at the rear of the building. I made it as far as the first hallway.

There I was stopped by two young ladies. One acted as spokes-woman for the other, whose tears gave her feelings away. "Brother Black, Marilyn needs to talk with you." Marilyn's tears increased.

I turned to Marilyn and said, "I would love to talk with you, but I have to be at the Salt Lake City International Airport by 4:10. I'll talk with you on Monday." My defense didn't work.

Still sobbing, Marilyn said, "It's so important. I need help. Now!"

Touched by her broken heart, I said, "Okay, but only for a moment. Come back to the office."

They did, and I asked what could possibly be so important. The core of the tragedy was almost beyond my twenty years of reasoning power gained in working with teenagers. Marilyn said, "Mike didn't say hello to me after this period today."

"What?" I said. "Mike didn't say hello to you today?"

This was the problem? This was what couldn't wait until Monday? Fortunately, my emergency reasoning power coupled with my emergency patience power, and I remained calm. The problem was serious to my young friend and so I began an intense discourse on man and his relationship with woman.

At the end of my mini-lecture/counseling session, during which we discussed possible reasons for Mike's behavior, Marilyn's tears subsided. She was soon ready to face the world again. But that little session took fifteen minutes. When I arrived at the airport I had the rare privilege of seeing the bottom side of my 737 aircraft as it flew over the highway.

My worst fears were confirmed when I found that the next flight to Los Angeles wouldn't arrive there until 6:50 P.M. I had to be at the L.A. harbor by 7:00 P.M. to catch the one and only chartered ferry to Catalina that evening. Even if, by some miracle, the next plane were on time, I knew there was no conceivable way I could get from the airport to the harbor in ten minutes. It would take ten minutes just to get from the gate outside. With no other alternative, however, I took the next plane, abandoning all hope of making my other connections.   Once in Los Angeles, I took a bus to my folks's home in Long Beach, and from there tried to call the youth conference leaders on Catalina. The youth were staying at a private YMCA camp, and the operator told me she had strict instructions not to trouble them except in the case of a death.

She said they were receiving too many calls from worried parents about their young ones being away from home for the first time.

Following my best attempts to change her mind, I finally hung up in discouragement. Suddenly, the phone rang. It was the sister from the camp calling me. She said she had discovered that my parents lived in Long Beach, and had hoped I might be there. She continued. "Listen carefully to these instructions. We can still get you here. There will be a sea plane leaving Long Beach airport in the morning at 7:30 a.m. Be on that plane. It will land in the Avalon Harbor, on the water, and pull up onto Rocky Beach Landing. There you will see a man with a red Volkswagen bus. Pay him fifty cents and ask him to take you to Point Mole. At Point Mole, there will be a man at the dock with a black speedboat."

"Wait a moment," I interrupted. "This is Don Black, not *James Bond!*"

She laughed, but not too hard, and immediately continued her instructions. "The man with the speed boat will take you directly to our camp on the north side of the island. That's all you need to do." I expected her to add, "This telephone will self-destruct in twenty seconds."

Early the next morning I was on my way. There were three seaplanes at the airport ready to take off. All three were sold out. The first started up and slowly taxied off. Then the second taxied down the runway. But there was one cancellation for the third plane, and I got it. What luck! We took off in that historical seaplane, Vintage 1939, and after a somewhat bumpy ride down the runway, we were airborne. A few low-flying minutes later, Catalina Island came into view, and we flew closer and closer to the sea. Finally, there was a thump, a sudden splash of water, and a rapid loss of speed. We instantly became a boat with projecting wings on either side. The whole thing was quite a thrill.

We maneuvered over to the beach area, and with a sudden burst of horsepower our boat pulled right out of the beautiful Pacific and onto the rocks of Rocky Beach Landing. I could see the red Volkswagen waiting in the background.

The small door opened, I grabbed my briefcase, and ran toward the bus. I handed the driver fifty cents, said, "Point Mole, please," and off we went. Three minutes later we were there. I got out, and immediately saw a man standing next to a black speedboat. "Are you Mr. Black?" he asked. I nodded. And he said, "This way, please."

I stepped cautiously into the black speedboat and we drove slowly out of the harbor. Then he opened up speed. We bounced up and down. Mist and sprays of the salty Pacific found their target—my face. I wondered what in the world I was doing in a suit and tie, bouncing around in a little speedboat.

At the northern side of the island there was a long, wooden dock that projected out from the shoreline and into the bay. My driver turned to me and yelled above the loud whine of the motor. "I can't bring this thing to the beach. You see that dock? When I pass by it, you jump onto a ladder on the side." I didn't dare say, "What?" I had heard him, and we were too close for any kind of debate. My heart was racing, though, as I felt more and more like the invincible Mr. Bond. I only hoped I had his luck. When we were close enough, the driver yelled, "Jump!" And I jumped!

There I was, clinging to the ladder, my feet being lapped by the Pacific Ocean, a briefcase in one hand and me holding as tightly as possible to the wet and slimy ladder with the other. I made my way to the top of the dock where the sister in charge of the youth conference greeted me as though nothing unusual had happened. "Welcome, Brother Black. This way, please."

She led me down the dock to the beach, up a grassy knoll, and through a little canyon trail. There before my eyes was a beautiful group of young people in an open amphitheater. They were singing those traditional sing-until-the-speaker-comes songs. After all of my adventures, I was only fifteen minutes late!

The program was divided into three separate seminars, with a different group of youth each hour. I was to give the same message to each group. During the third hour of presentation, however, something happened, and I found myself changing the contents of my talk drastically. The discussion became much more serious and searching. I sensed that something special, memorable was taking place. We could all feel it. We completed that highly spiritual third hour with our testimonies strengthened and renewed.

As the youth filed out for their lunch break, one woman came up to me and said, "I am one of the group leaders here at the youth conference, and I attended your three seminars. Your last talk was distinctively different from the other two. Why?"

"I'm not sure, " I confessed. "All I know is that the Spirit prevailed, and my thoughts and words went with it."

"That's marvelous," she replied. "There were certain youth in that particular group who needed exactly what you told them. It was an answer to our prayers, and one of our specific hopes for this conference."

On my speedboat ride back to Rocky Beach Landing, I pondered over and over again how I had almost missed this spiritual experience—not to mention the adventure. I gave special thanks at the first opportunity to a loving Heavenly Father.

And Monday, when I saw Mike in the hallway . . .

DON'T LEAVE TONIGHT

Certainly the Lord hears our prayers, and is aware of our needs. But usually he answers these prayers and responds to our needs through the service and actions and inspiration of others. I have learned that very often sincere and faithful people intervene at just the right moment to protect us, lead us, and help us meet our obligations. Perhaps they act as a Liahona to us when we are too preoccupied to consult the one within. I won't soon forget one experience that illustrates that principle.

It had been a late and tiring evening at the church. There had been several complicated interviews and counseling sessions. I still wasn't finished, but I was anxious to get home. I knew my family was waiting for me because we intended to begin our Thanksgiving trip to California that night.

As I ushered another person into my office for an interview, my first counselor in the bishopric motioned to me from the hallway. "Excuse me, Bishop," he said, "but can I see you for a moment?" I stepped out into the hallway and said quietly, "I have someone in the office just now. Can it wait?"

"No, it can't," he replied firmly. Then, placing his arm over my shoulder, he led me into an empty office nearby.

"What's going on?" I asked. "Is something wrong?"

"Yes, there is something wrong, Bishop. I just learned that you are planning to begin your vacation tonight, and you intend to drive all night to California. Is that true?"

"Yes," I said, "it is. It will give us nearly another full day to visit with our family there."

"Not really," he said. "You will be so tired upon arrival that you will probably spend most of that day sleeping. Bishop, I am going to say something to you now as your counselor. I feel you shouldn't leave tonight."

"Why not?" I questioned.

"Because it is not wise, and probably not safe. We need you. We need your family. I'm serious. I feel you should not leave tonight. And really, the time you would save won't make much difference."

I could see he was *very* serious. "Well," I said, "what about Ann and the kids? They will be very disappointed."

"Would you like me to call Ann?" my counselor offered.

"Yes, would you do that?" He said that he would, and he disappeared into another office to make the call while I returned to the person waiting in my office.

Later my counselor told me everything was taken care of, that Ann had put the children to bed and had agreed to leave in the morning. "Thanks," I said, "I really didn't want to drive all night."

Many times I've wondered about my counselor's serious admonition. I don't know that anything would have happened had we taken off across the Nevada desert late that evening. But I felt his promptings were not only sincere but well-founded. I trusted him.

Early the next morning we began our journey and found some of the mountain passes and roads snow-covered and icy. It was a challenge to hold the car steady as we drove over the dangerous highways, and we discussed how difficult things might have been in the dark night under heavy snowfall. That evening, upon our safe arrival in California, I found a quiet place and knelt to thank our Father for the inspired advice and guidance of my counselor and friend.

A HIGH WIRE AND A CLOSE CALL

We were out as a family, looking at carpeting. We drove into the parking area of a carpet store. As I found a parking space, Ann said, "Don! There is a man laying over there!" I looked, and sure enough, there lay a man, very still upon the ground. I asked her to watch the children and I jumped out of the car and ran to where the man lay. I could see he was a workman. There were other workmen in the area, and a large crane close by. The lone cable, ball and hook, were swinging back and forth near where the man lay. I reasoned it had swung around and accidentally hit the man on the head. The crane had been engaged in hoisting huge roof trusses to the top of the unfinished building next door.

By the time I reached the man, one of his coworkers had also arrived. The man was not breathing. His eyes were opened and looking directly into the sun. His friend immediately began mouth-to-mouth resuscitation. I grabbed his helmet and held it to shade his eyes. I noticed that the fingers of his gloves were severely burned. The long cable was swinging back toward us, and I reached out my hand to keep it from hitting us. I grabbed it and was pushing it on around the area where we stood.

At that same moment, one of the workmen in the distance yelled, "Don't touch that!" I couldn't imagine why he gave the warning, but I let go immediately. A moment later there was a loud crackling sound. It was right overhead.

I looked up and the reason behind the whole drama was suddenly made clear to my puzzled mind. The crane had swung around and hit a live, high-voltage wire above. The man had touched the cable and was electrocuted, thus the heavy burn marks on his gloves. The lone cable was still swinging back and forth.

I had grabbed onto the same cable. When I looked up, I saw that the cable had momentarily bounced off the high wire, and was just returning to it when I let go. It was more than a coincidental sequence, for when it touched again, there was another terrifying snapping sound.

This time the sudden charge of wild electricity ran down the steel girding of the crane with such force that it caused the tires on the crane to burst into flames. It was suddenly becoming a very dangerous and complex situation.

I looked at the crane. The operator was attempting to direct the cable away from the wire. He did not yet see the flames beginning to engulf the lower part of the unit. I yelled to him to get out. I could see the fuel tanks strapped to each side between the sets of tires. I knew we didn't have long before the whole area became an exploding inferno.

I yelled to Ann to drive the car and kids to safety behind the building. She did.

The man still lay on the ground, his friend working over him frantically. The crane was burning, with billows of black smoke beginning to fill the area. It was a frightening scene.

We stayed with the man, while I engaged in a whole lot of silent praying for his well-being and our safety. Finally, he began breathing!

We helped him to his feet and assisted him to a safer place on the other side of the parking lot.

A police car stopped and the policeman came running with a fire extinguisher in hand. With the aid of others who brought fire extinguishers he succeeded in controlling the blaze before the fuel tanks ignited.

When we drove home later, Ann and I talked about it. We had just sung at a funeral earlier that day. She said softly, "We as a family could be making plans right now for *your* funeral, Don. I'm so thankful you were protected."

So was I. It was too close. When I review the newspaper article about the incident, my thankfulness for life and for the guidance and protection of the Lord is recalled and appreciated all over again.

Chapter Nine

Satan's Arsenal vs. The Whole Armor of God

"Pray always, that you may come off conqueror; yea, that you may conquer Satan, and that you may escape the hands of the servants of Satan that do uphold his work." (D&C 10:5)

While fulfilling a research assignment in a religion class several years ago, I found a great source of information in section 10 of the Doctrine and Covenants. Woven throughout this revelation is one of the best and most detailed accounts of the Adversary's *modus operandi* I've discovered.

Many forthright warnings are given to us, and Satan's impressive arsenal is exposed. We see that he works with helpers who seek to destroy individuals and their gifts and talents. He uses every trick in the book, and then some—cunning, lies, temptation, deception, flattery, and ambush. The list of his weapons is detailed and complete.

This revelation, to the Prophet Joseph Smith in the summer of 1828, is a perfect and timely warning.

Too often, we don't understand or take heed of inspired warnings in our younger years. I know I didn't. This brings to mind a few experiences of my youth when wisdom was substituted with and replaced by poor judgment.

One such experience began after a date with a really attractive girl. I had just taken her home and was driving past the local drive-in. It was late and I shouldn't have stopped. But I noticed some of my friends, and pulled in anyway. They were having a hot discussion about whose car was the fastest. One of our friends owned a brand-new car. It had the biggest V-8 engine the factory built, plus an added racing accessory—the coveted supercharger. His opponent drove a one-year-old car with a hemi stick-shift.

The conversation persisted, and finally a challenge was made. My friend, who owned the new car, asked if I wanted to ride with him, and without any thought I answered, "Sure." We all headed for a two-mile section of nearby highway. There was a large field on the left and a big tire manufacturing company on the right. The long section of road was uninterrupted except at the end where there was a lonely and dark intersection.

Because the car we were in sported an automatic transmission, it was agreed that a moving start would be fair. We took our positions at the far end of the road and began moving slowly at about fifteen miles an hour. At the call of "go" the two big cars rolled like nothing I had ever experienced before. I instantly felt the fear of upcoming trouble.

Tires burned, smoked, and screamed as the silence and peace of the early-morning hour was shattered. The other car took a slight lead, then edged ahead more. I looked over at the speedometer. It was already hitting seventy, then eighty and ninety. I couldn't believe it. I could hear the distinct sound of the whistling, straining supercharger. But it had met its match in the hemi. We were nearing the end of the prearranged shut-off point. But it was apparent that no one was going to slow down. The race became deadly serious. The speeds grew dangerously faster. The intersection was approaching.

Then I saw him. An old man was driving home from the late shift. He had no idea those cars were approaching. After his stop, he proceeded slowly into the intersection. In split seconds we were upon him. I looked over at my driver, but there was no way to stop.

The other car entered the intersection first. He was to our right and swerved dangerously around the front of the old man's car. We were next. We swerved to the left and narrowly avoided a collision.

At that moment, I glanced over at the speedometer. It showed 103 miles per hour! I figured that our friend must have been going about 110. The old man had stopped in near shock right in the middle of the street. Had we hit him, it would have been a horrible collision of fire and twisted metal and bodies. I vowed silently that I would never be involved in such an activity again.

I later apologized to my Heavenly Father, and then thanked him for the miraculous deliverance. It was, without doubt, a cunning plan from Satan's arsenal to destroy us, and we had only narrowly escaped.

QUICKSAND

As a young man, I once went exploring with some friends in a wilderness area. We came to a large riverbed where the river was much smaller than the area it had to flow in, and we began walking the sandy banks. Suddenly, I began to feel my feet mysteriously sinking into the sand. At first I was able to easily remove each foot as I continued walking, but the farther I walked, the deeper my feet began to sink.

I had heard of quicksand, but had never been in or around it. I started to sink quickly as I walked—at first up to my ankles, then toward my knees. I changed my direction and headed for more solid ground. The sand pulled at my feet, but I continued slowly toward the safer, more secure ground and finally I made it.

I remembered my father had told me that when he was just a youth, he too had walked into the luring sands. He had been caught by the quicksand's power and had struggled until it had nearly covered his entire body. With only his neck and head above the deadly sands, a man had come by, handed him a long branch, and slowly pulled him to safety.

I considered the subtlety of such a trap. The sand looked like any other—soft, safe, and fun to run in. I thought of Satan and his similar method of luring people into his traps by making sin appear to be safe and fun. Why would anyone sin, if it was not alluring? Why would anyone sin if it was not fun—at first.

The allegory of the quicksand and Satan's method of trickery was worth pondering. Deception, flattery, and leaving the tried pathway of safety—it all matched up. I was grateful that I had heeded the warning signs and been saved from great physical danger, while also learning an important lesson about Satan's methods of deceit.

The Whole Armor–and Then Some

When traveling in Europe we went by third-class rail to the lovely little country village of Segovia in Spain. The center attraction in this medieval town is the castle used in the movie *Camelot*. It is precariously perched upon a precipice of sheer stone surrounded by water and a drawbridge, and is a most amazing sight.

During our visits we explored every hallway, room, and tower. We walked upon steps of solid stone. We sat where Columbus spoke to Queen Isabella regarding the ships needed for his great adventure. We could almost hear the tales of yore.

One set of towers in the castle was reserved for honored guests, and the opposite group of towers was for enemy prisoners. When we approached the dungeon of this historical stone edifice, we were greeted by rows of suits of armor. All types and sizes were represented. We saw full-sized models of horses equipped with the metal shroudings of protection. It appeared to me that there would be no way an enemy could render a blow effective enough to down someone so protected.

The suits of armor included breastplates that completely covered the vital areas of neck, chest, heart, and stomach. A shielding covered the legs and feet, arms and elbows, and warriors wore steel mace gauntlets to protect the hands and wrists. The headgear consisted of a complete covering, with a slitted visor over the eyes. There appeared to be total immunity from attack.

But on one particular row, my eyes caught a part of the story I had never seen before. As I walked *behind* the men of steel, I noticed the breastplates were completely open in the back. There were only cords of leather, binding the piece to the man's body. He would be totally vulnerable to an attack from this angle. All the enemy had to do was encircle the man and attack from behind.

This discovery caused me to ponder the admonition of Paul to put on the whole armor of God, and suddenly the rest of the warning filled my mind. After taking upon ourselves the whole armor of God, we need to keep our senses on full alert. Though armed, we must never turn our backs upon the enemy.

What a message to the members of the church, and to righteous people everywhere! What a vivid warning to us all! Although we have our membership, with its powers and blessings, we still must not turn our backs upon the enemy. We must constantly protect ourselves.

It's All Wrong—Pay the Tithing

How easy it is to allow a small chink in our armor—a chink that gives the Adversary a perfect opening for attack. While there are many such instances in my own life, one in particular comes to mind. The financial ramifications of the early days of marriage were frightening at times. It was difficult to make enough money to support my small and growing family, and then even more troublesome to try to handle what money we had successfully and prudently. At times I found if I wasn't extremely careful it was tempting to want to delay paying tithing while we caught up on other "more pressing" expenses. Clearly, this was dangerous reasoning for anyone who wanted to keep his financial obligations clear with the Lord. It's too easy to pay the Lord last, especially when He is the last to ask.

During the time since our early days of marriage, we've learned that paying tithing first somehow makes the other bills easier to pay—not harder. But some years ago, Ann and I caught ourselves slipping behind in our tithing payments. At the time, I thought we were justified, and promised to catch up later. But time slipped by, and unexpected expenditures came, and suddenly we were $225 behind in our tithing—which at the time was a measurable sum.

A few years previous we had owned a small retail store, and the purchaser still owed us a few payments. One day, unexpectedly, a check arrived from him. It was for $250. Seeing that much money in a lump sum had its immediate effect on me. I promptly began figuring all of the bills we could pay with that money—Penney's, Sears, the car insurance that was due, and a new battery and tires for the car. I was ecstatic.

That's when Ann sweetly said, "Let's pay our tithing."

I am still ashamed that I actually resisted the idea, suggesting we could catch up on our tithing when our income tax return arrived. Ann reminded me that if we waited, we would not be able to count ourselves as full tithe payers at the end of the year. I reasoned that a month or so could hardly make much difference. We never resolved things, and Ann went to bed while I stayed up to work out the intricacies of spending the $250. By midnight I'd written out the checks, addressed and sealed the envelopes, and prepared for bed.

Quietly I entered the bedroom so I wouldn't disturb Ann. When I realized I hadn't had evening prayer yet, I tiptoed out again and knelt in the living room. It was a beautiful, clear night, and the lights of the city glittered in the darkened sky. I was so exhausted that my prayer was short. Again, quietly, I entered the bedroom and went to bed.

The next thing I knew, I had been awakened. I still don't know if I heard a voice or simply had an impression strong enough to wake me. But these words came into my mind: "It's all wrong. Pay the tithing." The words startled me so much, and seemed so real, that I said, "What, dear?" There was no answer. Then I realized what was happening, turned immediately to Ann and awakened her. "Ann, it's all wrong."

I looked at the clock, remembered it was Sunday morning, and realized the bishop was probably already in his office. I jumped out of bed, called him, and asked if it was too late to arrange for tithing settlement. He assured me it wasn't, and we made an appointment for that same day. During the interview, when the bishop asked if we were full tithe payers, Ann and I looked at each other, smiled broadly, and said, "Yes sir. With this payment we are." It was a marvelous feeling.

The stack of unpaid bills were waiting for us when we arrived home, but I still felt good about our decision to pay the tithing first. Two days later a letter arrived from my parents in California. They asked if we were interested in selling them a little lakeside building lot we had purchased earlier. The amount they offered totaled almost exactly what we needed to pay off the bills once destined to be paid with the Lord's money.

Coincidence? I think not. In life, it pays to keep your account paid up with the Lord. And again, the admonition of Paul raced through my mind. We must put on the whole armor of God, never allowing the Adversary to overtake us from behind, to obscure good judgment and righteous intentions with rationalization or other tools Satan relies upon.

Chapter Ten

My Brother: A Man With "Greater Love"

"Greater love hath no man than this, that a man lay down his life for his friends." (JOHN 15:13)

For as long as I can remember, I felt that my brother, Richard, was an unusual person. A special person. Oh, some might wonder if my admiration wasn't simply that of a younger brother. And certainly there was some of that. But there were other things that went far beyond a little boy's awe.

Richard always seemed to have compassion for others, and he wasn't ashamed to show it. He was the one who would make the shy or unpopular person feel a part of the crowd. He was the first to stop if someone was in need.

On one such occasion, as he and several friends were returning from a camping expedition, they came upon an accident scene. Immediately they stopped to see if they could render aid. There were fresh tracks indicating that a vehicle had gone over the side of the narrow mountain road, and by this time the small crowd that had gathered was peering down the mountain to catch sight of the crashed vehicle.

Richard quickly learned that the crash victims were still in the vehicle, far below. When Richard asked what had been done to help them, the man answered by saying he'd heard that one individual died in the crash but that because of the treacherous terrain it would be too difficult to rescue the one who had survived.

At that remark, Richard became angry. He spotted a truck with a hydraulic winch on the front, found the owner and ordered him, "Bring it over here. Now!" The owner obeyed, pulling the truck to the edge of the cliff. Richard then loosened the cable on the power winch, wrapped it around his waist, and gave the signal to let it out slowly as he made his way carefully down the steep mountainside.

Upon reaching the wrecked Jeep, he found that one man had died. But the second was alive, and his leg was trapped under a corner of the Jeep. Richard motioned for his friends to join him, and one by one they came down the cable as Richard had. Together, they were able to lift the Jeep off the man's leg, and then begin their way back up the mountain.

It was an exhausting climb. Their lungs burned as they struggled to propel themselves upward, as well as lift the injured man. They stopped frequently to catch their breath and rest. Eventually, all made it to the top. That man, previously a stranger to Richard and his friends, lives today. It is incidents like this one that reinforced within me a sense of deep awe for my brother.

Richard loved the outdoors. He was never as happy as when he was camping, hiking, or backpacking far away from the sights and smells of the nearest city. Eventually, he moved his family to the little mountain community of Silverado Canyon, California. Their home was on the side of a mountain, and he and his boys would frequently climb the big mountain behind their home. They loved it.

One day after they'd moved to Silverado, Richard called our mother just to tell her how much he loved her. The call proved to be a tender experience for both. It wasn't long after, in the middle of the night, Richard awakened suddenly. He was sweating profusely and crying out, "It's coming down. It's coming down. The mountain is coming down on me." His wife, Sally, tried to comfort him, but the dream had been so realistic that he couldn't get it out of his mind.

About this time, southern California was hit extremely hard with violent rainstorms that didn't quit. During one stretch it rained for nearly a week without letting up. The threat of flooding was a reality for thousands of residents. The usually picturesque creek that flowed near Richard's home turned into a raging torrent. And the rains continued.

At first, only small homes near the river were flooded. Then some highways were totally covered with water and huge sections of roadway began to break away, washing downstream, then down the canyon. With each day, the continued rain produced yet another nightmare. Richard and Sally watched a home just across the street tilt up and over into the dangerous sweeping current of uncontrolled water. They saw other homes demolished before their eyes. Their car was swept away. Preservation, even survival, became an all-consuming worry.

Richard and many others like him spent their days sandbagging and helping those in need. Richard joined the volunteer fire department, often assisting those unable to help themselves out of the canyon. Marine helicopters nearby flew mercy missions in and out of the flooded areas.

With the press of survival, Richard and others worked days on end with little sleep. During one stretch he and a neighbor had worked forty-two hours straight until their bodies were numb with fatigue and cold. Finally, at midnight one night, Richard came home for some rest. He found a number of homeless people occupying his house—to the point that there was no bed for him to sleep in.

Sally hung his wet Army coat in front of the fireplace to dry—no utilities were functional—and Richard slumped himself in a vacant chair in the living room. At 2:00 a.m. he jumped up and said, "Sally, where's my coat. I've got to get back out there." She tried to persuade him to rest a little longer, but he could not be deterred. There were too many people who still needed help, he explained, slipping on his still-damp jacket, kissing Sally good-bye, and walking back out into the dark and wet night.

The next evening the phone rang at my home. I was a little surprised when it was Dad. It was usually Mother who called, and Dad would say a quick "hello" or call from the background, "Say hello to my boy and his family." But this night he had placed the call, and the minute he said, "Son," I sensed a different tone in his voice and responded, "Dad? Is everything all right?"

There was a long pause. Finally he said, "Don, your brother was killed today. Mom needs you badly. How soon could you come home?"

The shock of those words pushed me back against the doorway as though I'd been physically pushed. I couldn't believe what I'd heard. "Dad, I didn't hear you. What did you say?" When he repeated the message, my body and feelings went numb. Then everything began to ache. I wanted to cry, but tears wouldn't come. But how it hurt! I mumbled that I'd make arrangements immediately, then hung up, turned to my wife, and told her.

Memories began to flash through my mind. I pictured Richard grasping the straps of his backpack, his long legs taking giant strides as we hiked up a mountain. I remembered the times we'd laughed together, the times we'd told jokes as we fell asleep in a tent in the wilderness country, the times I'd seen him cry. I started to remember all the times I'd seen him perform some act of kindness. I thought about the man whom he'd rescued from the overturned Jeep. How I loved my brother!

I'd been so stunned by the news I hadn't even asked Dad how it happened. I supposed it had something to do with all of the rescue work he'd been doing, but there was no time for speculation now. We had to make immediate preparations to leave for California. That drive from Utah seemed to be the longest I had ever taken. When I arrived at my parents' home, the strangest feeling of emptiness came over me. It would never be the same again.

Mother didn't look well. As I took her in my arms and held her close, she sobbed. As we held each other we talked softly about the reassurances of the gospel. At that heartbreaking moment, all we had to hold onto was each other and the gospel plan.

Later that day I learned how Richard had died. He and a neighbor had been transporting an injured teenage boy on a stretcher to a fire station, where he would be picked up by a Marine helicopter. They got the boy to the back room of the fire station, but because they were so tired they weren't able to carry him ten more feet to the front of the building. They had reached a point of exhaustion.

Then it happened. It's likely that they felt the tremor and could hear the deep rumbling as the soggy mountain began to come down. A giant landslide of mud, debris, rocks, and trees crashed through the back wall of the fire station. The neighbor working alongside Richard described what happened. "I saw your brother look at that boy lying on the stretcher, and instinctively throw his body down over him. They were almost immediately buried in the muck. The force of the slide was great enough to push me out through the front of the building. I survived, though, and I knew approximately where your brother and the boy had been buried. So when it all stopped, we immediately began to dig.

"When I came to your brother, I instantly knew that he had died. But the boy under him was alive! He saved the boy's life!"

It was then the tears came for me. How like him, I thought. As much as it hurt to have my brother gone, how appropriate for his last act to have been one in which he put someone else's welfare above his own.

It was the next day that Mom asked me if I would speak at Richard's funeral. I didn't want to add to her grief, so I answered, "Of course, Mom." But inside I was crying, How can I possibly speak about my brother when I can't even think about it without the tears flowing?

During the time between then and the funeral, I begged the Lord to give me strength. I knew, in and of myself, I did not have the energy or the ability to say what would be appropriate. My mind and heart were filled with feelings about Richard. Because of his death I felt that I understood a little better the atoning sacrifice of our Savior, the giving of His life for others. I received the clear impression that Richard wanted his sons and wife to know that he'd done what he had to do, and that there should be no regrets.

The day of the funeral I was able to keep my emotions in check until I took my place on the stand and noticed the banners on certain flower arrangements. One read, "To my brother." Another, " To my husband." Another, "To our daddy." And then there was the one from Mom and Dad: "To our son." At the sight of that one, my emotions were suddenly unleashed. I broke down, hiding myself behind one of the large floral arrangements.

Later, when I spoke, I was blessed with the strength and composure to deliver my brief message. As hard as it was, I was proud to honor my brother. As I stood at the pulpit I couldn't help but be impressed with the variety of people who'd come to pay their respects to Richard—people whom he'd touched in his life. There were returned missionaries and church leaders. The African-Americans, Hispanics, and Japanese sat intermingled with Caucasians. There were men and women elegantly dressed, and others who looked to be throwbacks to the hippie era. One young man had even been allowed to come from prison to attend the funeral.

On the way out, I noticed an African-American couple walking just in front of me. The man was weeping, his head bowed low. I placed my arm around his shoulder and said softly, "Thank you for coming to my brother's funeral." The man looked up, and with tears flowing from his reddened eyes said, "He was my brother, too. He was my brother, too."

Richard was a brother to a lot of people. He was a man as Christ so amply described, " . . . with greater love." I miss him, but can't wait until that glorious day of the resurrection when we will have that opportunity to see him again, and be nurtured by his presence. I am comforted and consoled in the Savior's words: "But behold, verily I say unto you, before the earth shall pass away, Michael, mine archangel, shall sound his trump, and then shall all the dead awake, for their graves shall be opened, and they shall come forth—yea, even all" (D & C 29:26).

Thank thee, Father, for the miracle of the resurrection and for all thine other miracles, large and small that can fill our lives with comfort and with joy.

About the Author

Don J. Black, educator and counselor, is best known for his extra-ordinary ability to touch the hearts of readers and listeners with true stories. He is the author of many books and articles and has produced numerous outstanding talk tapes for Covenant Recordings. His love of youth has resulted in many awards such as the Distinguished Service Award and the Outstanding Youth Leader of America Award. He has served as a bishop, and presently is a psychotherapist in Mesa, Arizona where he resides with his wife, Ann, and their four children.